WORK *as* WORSHIP

low the CEOs of Interstate Batteries, Hobby Lobby, PepsiCo, Tyson Foods and more, bring meaning to their work

Mark L. Russell, Editor

Foreword by:
Dave Gibbons

Introduction by:
Brian Mosley

Contributions from:

Mo Anderson, Dennis Bakke, Howard Dahl, Ken Eldred, David Green, Scott Harrison, Henry Kaestner, Blake Lingle, Brian Lewis, Steve Lynn, Edwin Meese III, David W. Miller, Norm Miller, Blake Mycoskie, Steve Reinemund, Jeffrey A. Russell, Tyler Self, John Tyson, and JR Vassar

Boise, Idaho

Portions of this book were previously published in the title *Our Souls at Work: How Great Leaders Live Their Faith in the Global Market-place.*

Published in Boise, Idaho by Russell Media

Web: http://www.russell-media.com

Bulk discounts are available for ministry, educational, business, or promotional use.

For information please email info@russell-media.com.

ISBN (print): 978-1-937498-02-3

ISBN (e-book): 978-1-937498-03-0

Cover design and layout by Drew Steffen.

Printed in the United States of America.

CONTENT

WORK AS WORSHIP
FOREWORD

FOREWORD by DAVE GIBBONS

It was the day of my mother's funeral; the day every child dreads and has nightmares about. It actually happened. As a second-year university student, I received a phone call that my mom was killed in a hit-and-run accident.

In the memorial service, I sat in disbelief as the room filled with family and friends. My father did not attend because he had recently finalized the divorce and remarried. It would have been awkward for him. It was my sister, my brother, and myself on the front row looking at my mom lying in a casket. The moment was surreal, accentuated by utter terror that Mom was gone. My mother had worked and sacrificed so much for us. She once said, "The only reason I live is for you children." Since the divorce, Mom's life had spiraled out of control. Her American dream had become a living nightmare. The house, swimming pool, new cars, boats, and trips didn't mean much to her after she and dad went their separate ways.

In the midst of the pain and what seemed to be a funeral service in slow motion, I felt I heard God saying to me, "Dave, on this earth there are things that are temporal and things that are eternal. The things that you desire don't mean much in light of eternity. I want you to give yourself completely to me and focus your life to serve me."

I translated that to mean God wanted me to go into ministry. This would be full surrender! In my mind, full surrender was full-time dedication to serving God as a pastor in a church not in a "secular" business in the world. Reluctantly, and with great resignation, I told God, "Okay, I will do it." At that moment, my journey to understanding what God meant had begun, while at the same time, an inner sense that I had a calling to business grew. I tried to quiet the conviction, but a deep inner conflict kept growing. I didn't know what to do with these seemingly incongruous feelings. How could I serve God fully other than as a minister? I buried this calling to business as a "worldly" or "secular" desire that I had to squash in order to stay obedient to what I thought was the true calling of full-time ministry. The spiritual leaders in my life told me that this ministerial calling was the highest and truest calling of all.

The Great Divide

Now, almost thirty years later, I think I have a fuller understanding of what God was trying to say to me as a young, passionate activist. The spiritual context I grew up in was a black and white environment. In an age of relativism, clear black and white posturing—theologically or politically—was common. The gravitational pull to simplicity and dogmatism seemed reactionary to what many feared was "liberalism" or "secularism" creeping into the church. Absolutes and clear lines of distinction were craved by a generation whose tenets of faith were being challenged by society.

The tone of spiritual conversation frequently drew upon war metaphors. While I know this is how Paul spoke in the New Testament, there are other metaphors of love and community that are also used. Again, not to condemn this generation's pursuit of Jesus, but I believe this is how the current rhetoric was shaped when it came to being fully surrendered to Jesus. In fact, I remember asking the senior minister one time, "Is everything so black and white in the Bible?" He said, "Yes."

What does this mean to those who are called to serve God outside of the church, or other than as traditional ministers?

Quite frankly, there was a difference for us between those who gave up all to go into "full-time ministry" and those who simply provided support to us in "full-time ministry." The secular and the sacred were distinct categories. Moreover, faith and work, while discussed, never really converged. Unfortunately, those who had regular nine-to-five jobs weren't really doing sacred work unless they served in the church. Is it any wonder that those who are not pastors only feel appreciated for their financial gifts and not for who they are as people?

In the global shifting that is going on today, the concerns are commonly economic and political in nature. However, the biggest concern should be the under-utilization of the human resources in our midst, those who comprise the church we go to every Sunday. There is a need for the priesthood, the body of Christ to arise. The normal every day businessperson, mother, student, worker need to see themselves at the frontline of what God is doing in the world. They should not be simply following the pastors; they are the ones called to lead.

The truth is that faith and work do intersect. In fact, all is sacred to God. Paul says, "Whether you eat or drink, or whatever you do, do all to the glory of God" (1 Corinthians 10:31 ESV). The highest calling is not being a pastor but becoming all God called you to be, namely a person who glorifies God in all you do.

The word *glory* conveys the idea of beauty. So as we do good work that reflects God's character graciously, purely, morally, ethically, creatively, and excellently, we unleash his beauty. People see God. Our work is a way to worship God. It has intrinsic value and can demonstrate God's character when we do *good* work. Faith and work are to be seamless. Work is an expression of our life in Christ. Separating the two is like separating *being* from *doing*. How do you know who you are *being* without considering what you are *doing*—or the fruit you are producing your life?

I am genuinely thrilled about the wisdom made available in this book, *Work as Worship*. A new priesthood is rising up that must understand who they really are and who they are called to become. This book will provide needed guidance and an astute perspective into how the Kingdom of God can be made relevant to all people at all times in all places. My hope is this book will catalyze the new prophets that aren't just concerned about a single bottom line, but rather a *multiple* bottom line. It's a group who doesn't only want to make a profit, but aims to make a difference! It's a wave of global leaders who aren't going to let pastors have all the fun. It's a growing movement of zealots who see themselves on the front lines of God's campaign, no longer confined to warming the bench on Sunday mornings. This is a generation of leaders who know they're called to do more than give money, but everything they have. They are not going to miss out on one of the greatest moments in history to be alive!

My prayer, as you read this book, is that the Holy Spirit will give you a clear vision of who you are as a passionate worshipper unleashing the beauty of God in all that you do at work, at home, in the church, and in the world at large. You can't separate what you do from who you are. Your work *is* your worship. So worship God with all your heart, soul, mind, and strength. Unleash his beauty beyond the four walls of your church and into all of the domains you serve in the world.

Dave Gibbons
November 2011

WORK AS WORSHIP
INTRODUCTION

INTRODUCTION by BRIAN MOSLEY

I have a confession. I have been telling an incomplete story.

People are drawn most often to stories that involve conflict, drama and even some sensationalism. That's why People Magazine and TMZ are so popular.

I lead a ministry called RightNow that helps people have an "others before self, Christ above all" attitude. We've been able to serve over 100,000 churches through our video resources, live leadership events and online training. A big way our ministry accomplishes our mission is by telling people's stories. I bet our team has filmed over 1,000 stories in the past 10 years.

Storytellers are always looking to tell the best story possible. But sometimes in our pursuit of the "best" story we create an "incomplete" story. Here's what I mean.

If you asked most people in the church what kind of "ministry" they are doing, chances are they would give you a ministry activity that shows up on their calendar:

I teach a Bible study on Tuesday mornings.
I volunteer with YoungLife on Monday nights.
I am going on a mission trip in June.
I tutor kids on Thursday afternoons.

These are all great ministries and ministry can certainly happen as a scheduled event on a calendar. But if we only see ministry as something that we can schedule, then we have an incomplete picture.

I believe people have this view of ministry because of the stories we are telling. Most of the stories that we (church leaders) highlight about ministry involve the missionary overseas, the Young-Life volunteer, or the team that feeds the homeless. These stories are dramatic, powerful and sometimes even sensational because of the visible results—200 people came to Christ on that mission trip; that drug-addicted teen turned their life around; over $15,000 was raised for the project. These are great stories and they are fun to tell. But if we only tell these kinds of stories, we fail to show people that ministry can happen in the everyday pathways of life too.

I have been guilty of this. As I look back at the stories our team has captured in the past 10 years, we have showcased a lot of people doing incredible ministry that shows up somewhere on their calendar.

Then we had a revelation. Our stories might be conditioning people to think of ministry as a compartmentalized part of life instead of as being woven through all of life.

As we do life, you and I spend most of our waking hours in two places:

1. With our family
2. At work

I haven't met anyone who doesn't want to have a meaningful impact on their family. Helping people practice their faith at home is a high priority for many churches.

But knowing how our faith intersects with our work is more challenging.

Over the past two years, our RightNow team has started filming powerful stories of men and women who are living out their faith in and through their work. We believe these stories can inspire and validate the millions of Christians who go to work each day.

For you and the millions of other business leaders, your mission is in the marketplace. You may not be the kind of missionary who moves to the far regions of Africa. But around the conference table, around the water cooler, or around the cubicle, you have an opportunity to worship the God who created you.

He gave you skill. He gave you passion. He gave you work. When you do your job with excellence, integrity and diligence, it's an act of worship. You are displaying God's craftsmanship to the non-believing world around you. You are earning the right to be heard.

You don't see a divide between Sunday and Monday—between the sacred and the secular. You've been invited into parts of the world that a pastor or traditional missionary will never see. You have conversations with people who would never set foot in a church.

Church is not the only place you worship, and Sundays are not the only days on your calendar that have meaning.

God has designed you.

He created you to Work and to Worship.
For you, Work is Worship.

Here at RightNow, our chief champion for this idea that we call "work as worship" is Justin Forman, my Executive Vice President and a friend for over 10 years. On this two-year journey, Justin and I have met faithful business owners, entrepreneurs and executives who feel "called" to business. Mark Russell is one of those incredible leaders who crossed our path.

Mark shares our passion for highlighting the stories of those men and women who are in the trenches building their businesses while being faithful to Jesus.

Mark's expertise is print and ours is media. This book is the best of both worlds. Mark has interviewed some top-notch leaders and woven their insights together in this book. Throughout the pages you will also discover links to a handful of video stories that showcase additional leaders and companies.

Hopefully these stories will give us a bigger and broader picture of how God intends for us to worship in ALL that we do—including our work.

We want business leaders to know that their work matters and that your "calling" to the marketplace has value in the Kingdom.

Brian Mosley
President, RightNow

October 2011

CHAPTER ONE
CALLING

"God blessed them and said to them, 'Be fruitful and increase in number; fill the earth and subdue it. Rule over the fish of the sea and the birds of the air and over every living creature that moves on the ground.' "

Genesis 1:28

Calling is a complex and confusing topic for most people. As an ordained minister, I have been introduced on more than one occasion as someone who has a special call from God. While I do think I have a special call from God, I do not view a "special call" as synonymous with ordained ministry, which is the unfortunate implication of the introduction.

In the church, we have been conditioned to accept certain things; one of those is that clergy, church staff, missionaries, and those types of people have callings from God. Frequently this "call" from God takes these people out of the marketplace and into "ministry."

However, I have a long list of friends who say they have been called by God to leave the church and go back to work in the marketplace. Could that possibly be correct? Could God really call people to work in a mundane, "non-ministry-related" job? Isn't a call from God reserved for something more holy and higher than that?

As one who has been a pastor, a missionary, a seminary professor, and an entrepreneur, I can attest that it's all pretty mundane a lot of the time. I have come to believe that my "ministry" is wherever God "calls" me at any point in time. One thing I know for sure is that God calls us to many different places—and that he is calling us *all* to follow him wherever we are.

In the first recorded talk between God and humans, God called human beings to steward the earth's resources. Things have developed since that first conversation and contemporary work, though it certainly does not always reflect God's will and purposes, is still a divinely appointed process through which we fulfill that first calling. Business, far from being a necessary evil, is a vital part of God's mission in the world and is holy ground for those who follow Christ. We just need to recognize it as such.

In this chapter you will read from seasoned executives and business people, who in large part had to develop their own understanding of what is meant by "calling," and through their walk with Christ, have come to realize that business is indeed a worthy call.

J R VASSAR on
WORK AS WORSHIP

We know that whatever God is going to do, he is going to do it through his people. As the pastor of Apostle's Church in Manhattan, I believe that if we are going to advance the mission of Jesus, church leaders must commit to putting the mission in the hands of God's people.

I fear that much of what the church is equipping people for their personal lives and for ministry within the walls of the church. I am convinced that God's people must be equipped for their greatest missional context—their vocations.

People often see their job as a distraction from true ministry. There are 168 hours in a week. Most people are in church for only 1 to 3 hours. We will accelerate the mission of Jesus when we equip and encourage people for mission during the hours they spend away from the church, in their communities and their workplace.

But before people can live on mission in the marketplace, it's important that we have a biblical understanding of how God views work. In Genesis we learn that God is a worker and we were created in his image (Gen 2:4). God gave the mandate that man should arrange the raw materials of creation for the flourishing of the human community (Gen 2:15). Work is good, but deeply affected by the fall (Gen 3:17–19). Work is not simply a means; in some respects it is an end — an expression of being made in the image of

God. God has made us to work. So we need his wisdom on it.

There is a theology of work spelled out in the New Testament that shows how God is redeeming all of created life—even our work lives (Eph 6:5–9). For the sake of clarity, the word "slave" in this passage is not talking about 18th–19th century slavery, but rather slavery as defined in the 1st century Greco-Roman world. A slave, in that context, was someone who worked for and was compensated by another person who had absolute authority over his or her life. Our contemporary application of this passage is in the modern workplace — how we view and do our work as those who supervise and are supervised others.

Work is Worship

Your work is to be done to the Lord. How you perform tasks and supervise people is to be an act of worship (Eph 6:7–8). Christianity creates no division of secular and sacred. Every task we undertake, paid or not paid, is to be done to the Lord. Your job — whether you are building something, cooking a meal, changing a diaper, or sweeping the floor — is for his pleasure and is done in his presence. Part of worshiping through work is simply giving thanks for his provision.

If work is to be worship, it must also be excellent. God longs to put his people in positions of influence—for his glory—but there must be an increasing dependence upon the Holy Spirit for excellence before he'll open that door. We can't reduce the Spirit to simply helping us pray or preach or witness or behave. God can also give creativity and guidance to us as he told Moses he did to Bezalel (Ex 31:1–6). The Holy Spirit can give wisdom in solving problems, making wise decisions, and in dealing with crisis at work and in doing so, elevate you to places of influence within your workplace (Prov 22:29).

Work as worship but don't worship work

Our identity is in a Person, not in a position. We are the Lord's prized possession, bought with a price and called now to ultimately serve his purposes (Eph 6:5–6). We may have earthly bosses, but a heavenly Lord. We may be bosses but we have a Master in heaven (Eph 6:9). You are not to primarily see yourself in light of what you do before people, but in light of how you are loved by God.

You will not find what your soul truly craves by working for it, but by looking to Christ (John 6:27). This is why Sabbath is important (Heb 4:8–11). Resting from your labor teaches you that you are not a "some-body" or have value because of what you accomplish, but because of what God has accomplished and made you in Christ.

Work is an opportunity for the Gospel

Regardless of your vocation or your location, your mission is to be the sent people of God who display the presence, words and actions of God to the world. There is beauty and brokenness in our various industries and you can be used to foster transformation in your field. When you demonstrate the Kingdom, people benefit and humanity flourishes.

I am committed to creating space for this conversation at Apostle's Church. I want to help business people create networks that strive to demonstrate the Kingdom in their vocation domains. And I want to help disciple them for their public and professional lives.

Recently, we had a special service at Apostle's Church where we talked about neighborhoods, networks and nations. I asked Jamie, one of our church members who is an educator in the New York City school system, to share about how he's trying to put the Kingdom of God on display. This is what he said:

My vocation in education becomes not about teaching kids to pass tests, but promoting their flourishing as persons by seeking to shape their characters as well as their minds. It means creating classrooms of community and peace; restoring a vocabulary that includes words like mercy, compassion, forgiveness and justice. Tilling the soil of their hearts in hopes that the Spirit would plant faith.

Art becomes not just about selling paintings but imagining a world to come, sights unseen, making the invisible visible, and integrating words like truth and beauty back into the conversation. It's inciting a desire in the heart to search for the deeper and more beautiful truths of God.

Retail and marketing becomes not about buying and selling, but about humbly and joyfully serving people well. Lawyers work to see justice done and the innocent protected. Chefs remind us of God's abundant goodness in the delicacies they prepare.

The Gospel makes office politics becomes less about advancing my status and guarding my reputation and more about seeking the good of my co-workers, even the ones I don't like. We stay late, not in hopes of a promotion but to help someone struggling to finish their work.

As people of peace, we foster reconciliation between co-workers, offer counsel and comfort because Christ brought us counsel and comfort in abundance. We willingly labor, often in obscurity, so our actions and words might reintroduce the language of the Gospel into our workplace. We would be people of mercy, forgiveness, humility and wisdom.

What you are doing in your vocation matters. Leverage your vocation for worship and witness. That is how we will advance the mission.

Download a free sermon that JR Vassar gave on Work as Worship here: *www.rightnow.org/wawbook*

DENNIS BAKKE on
THE PURPOSE OF SECULAR WORK

What is the purpose of our daily work?

For those of us who are followers of Christ, we know our purpose is to be holy and glorify God. Many of us interpret "glorifying God" as making known his Kingdom and his ways. So how does our workplace fit into such a purpose? Should our workplace be our primary mission field where we seek, through word and deed, to carry out the Great Commission? Is it simply a means to provide for our families and earn enough extra to support our church, missions, and parachurch organizations? Or could it be secular work, even for-profit business, is the principle mission of ministry to which God calls many of us?

I have had the wonderful opportunity over the last twenty-five years to undertake various types of work. Which one do you think was most important to God?

- Nine years coaching youth league football
- The Mustard Seed Foundation—cumulative giving to Christian ministries and scholarships around the world exceeding $80 million
- Ten years as Sunday school teacher, head of missions, and chairman of deacons in our local church
- Twenty years leading a for-profit company (AES Corporation) that served the energy needs of more than 100 million people in thirty-one countries
- Leading a secular nonprofit (Imagine Schools) that operates seventy-three charter schools educating 35,000 students annually—the largest such organization in the nation

Which of these works is most important in God's perspective? Which is most consistent with serving God? Which best served my neighbor as myself?

When I left graduate school for government work in Washington, DC, thirty-nine years ago, my own understanding of work was to earn a living so I could give as much money and time as possible to the church and Christian ministry-related organizations. My high school math teacher exemplified this perspective. In my senior year, she asked me, "Dennis, what are you going to do with your life?" Like any high school senior, I didn't know and gave her the safest answer, "I really don't know, but I am planning to go to college." She had an agenda and replied, "I have some advice for you. Both your older brother, Ray, and your younger brother, Lowel, are committed to be pastors. Someone needs to support them."

She almost perfectly reflected my understanding of the vocational hierarchy available to Christians. The first priority, of course, was to be a missionary to Africa; second, a pastor; third—if you could do neither of those things—you might work for a Christian organization or school; fourth, some kind of service profession such as a doctor, social worker, or advocate. If, however, you weren't spiritual or gifted enough, you could go into business to support those at the top of God's pyramid. While few of us admit to the existence of any such hierarchy, it still seems very much alive in our churches and Christian schools.

Early in the 1980s, my wife and I joined a small group in our local church. One topic we studied was what the Bible said about work and the organizations in which we worked. This was timely for me. I found that God had a very different perspective than what I'd been previously taught. I learned that Genesis tells us God gave us a job even before he gave us a family. We were created in the image of God to be co-creators with him. That's how we glorify him. And that work was to be sublime, joyous, and sacred. Garden work, where we managed or had dominion over creation, was to be our primary mission when the world was still perfect.

What happened in the Garden? Man messed up God's work plan. Sin entered the world and work got harder, but it is not cursed. If anyone thinks work is cursed, they won't have the right attitude. Christ came to redeem work in us. By implication, it seems to me that we who are redeemed are supposed to be co-redeemers of work, to make our ordinary secular work as close as possible to the purposeful, joyous work that God gave us in the Garden, knowing that the redeeming process will not be complete until Christ returns.

Most of the work carried out by biblical heroes was secular:

- Noah was a shipbuilder, a zookeeper, and a cruise-line captain;
- Abraham was a real estate developer;
- Esther was a pageant winner so she could enter a harem before she became a queen;
- Daniel went to Harvard, the King's college, and became president of Iraq.

Most of us are called to secular workplaces, not primarily as evangelists or disciplers, but like these folks in the Bible, our job is to serve the ordinary needs of society as well as our own. Our work is to serve others and along the way our own needs will be met. That's what the great commandment says, "'Love the Lord your God with all your heart, and with all your soul and with all your mind' . . . and . . . 'Love [serve] your neighbor as yourself'" (Matthew 22:37, 39).

Joseph is an Old Testament prototype of Christ. God called Joseph to serve as the Chief Operating Officer of Cairo, Incorporated. In Joseph's secular working role, he probably saved thousands of people from starving to death, only a few of which were family members or followers of Yahweh. He was called to help feed the people, not make them disciples.

What does the New Testament say? Jesus spent eighty-five percent of his working life as a carpenter. The root word for carpenter is *tekton*, which has similar roots to the word "technology." Since there was very little wood in the area, Jesus was probably not a builder of cabinets or other wood products. Research has found the city of Sepphoris was being built around that time, and that Jesus and Joseph likely had jobs as stone masons building homes and other structures for the Greeks and Romans, not necessarily Jewish folks. Jesus probably spent most of his work life as a secular builder in a for-profit business. That is the model most of us should be following.

HOWARD DAHL on
THE SACRED / SECULAR DICHOTOMY

When we started Concord in 1977, I wrote my vision for the business. A few points were central to the vision. There was to be no sacred/secular dichotomy. It is important to see all of life as sacred, every detail. My father deeply influenced this viewpoint. He looked at all employees as being of equal value to a company and lived that out in his business practice. There are no small people. We've worked hard to make sure that all of our people are treated as equal members of the company.

Honoring the belief that everyone is of equal value is part of the ongoing conversation I have with our employees. I do a quarterly employee breakfast or lunch where I treat our staff as members of the board of directors. I update them on what's going on in the company, field their questions and listen to their input. Any employee that wants to talk to me personally can. We're small so this is easier to do than in a huge company. We've had a lot of meaningful conversations, and, over the years, many professions of faith.

We also have a lot of employee development programs focused on wellness. Last year, we brought in a nutritional coach to meet with employees individually. It's important to focus on the well-being of our people. If there's one thing that has governed our business, it's the Golden Rule, "Do to others what you would have them do to you."

DAVID MILLER on
THE THEOLOGY OF WORK

One of my favorite quotes from Martin Luther King, Jr. is, "If a man is called to be a street sweeper, he should sweep streets even as Michelangelo painted, or Beethoven composed music, or Shakespeare wrote poetry. He should sweep streets so well that all the hosts of heaven and earth will pause to say, 'Here lived a great street sweeper who did his job well.'" It's not necessarily what we do, but how we do it. There are redemptive purposes in knowledge worker jobs, skilled labor, and unskilled labor. There are a few points about the theology of work that we should keep in mind.

We are co-creators with God. Think of it as a partnership. Don't forget that God is the managing partner, and we are the junior partners, but we co-create with God. The work is not done.

To work is part of humanity. It is part of human anthropology and the doctrine of humanity. It is part of who we are and what we were created to do. I have yet to see someone who has stopped working, in the paid work sense, and after the first ninety days of playing unlimited golf and tennis, doesn't miss some aspect of the work, if they haven't found new co-creative activities to put their work skills into.

There is a time and a season for everything. (Ecclesiastes) Let us not forget that sometimes work is hard, boring, and monotonous; and sometimes work is easy, joyous, and invigorating. God can be present in both scenarios, if we remember to invite God in. You may be called, for a season, to be in a place that is pretty crummy, and there you are meant to be salt and light for a time. Work honorably and in a God-pleasing way. Hopefully, God will bless you then with a season where work is invigorating and stimulating, where you feel God's creative juices coming out of your fingertips.

Sometimes we are rewarded for our work and acknowledged publicly, and other times we are not. Just as Jesus taught us to pray very privately, and not to show off and brag in front of others, I think we ought to continue to do our work well whether we are rewarded financially and verbally in public or not. Two things matter: both what we do and how we do it. Some jobs are obviously making this creation into a better place, with a more obvious relationship to the coming kingdom of God. In other jobs, it is harder to make that connection. But God can be present in both.

Work is both a means and an end to honor God and serve our neighbor. Work is a form of worshipping God and serving neighbor, pulling together both the vertical and horizontal axis. If we hold this together, we can avoid the extreme of demonizing work on one hand or idolizing it on the other. That's the essence of the Jewish word *Avodah*, and the reason I gave The Avodah Institute that name. The root word for *Avodah* is translated in the Hebrew Scriptures differently, based on the context, it can mean "work," "worship," and "service." Whatever our places and kinds of work may be, our work matters deeply to God. We have a calling right in front of us.

KEN ELDRED on
THE "CALLING" MYTH

When it comes to business as usual, godly traits tend to be overlooked, and nothing seems absolute. Knowledge is increasing at such fantastic rates that we don't have time to learn it all. The world has brought us new thought processes, and because we often don't have time to stop and reflect, we automatically adopt them as our own. So it is with business and common conventions. We buy into them because we hear them over and over again, not because we have seen them proven true.

Churches don't necessarily teach the importance of business from a scriptural perspective, and so we end up operating on conventional wisdom. The idea of myths is not new. In the parable of the talents, the one who buried the talent did so operating under a myth. When the king called the man to account, he replied with a myth about God saying in essence: I knew you were a terrible tyrant reaping where you did not sow. (See Luke 19:20-21.)

Myths can ruin your whole understanding of God and what you are called to do. There are a lot of myths that need busting. Here's one:

Committed Christians should go into ministry.

This is a serious issue for people. As a child, my parents dropped me off at church in the morning, and I walked home without going in. It didn't mean a lot to me then. As I grew up, church and the things of God continued to mean very little to me. By the time I got to business school, my whole objective there was to finish, not to reflect on any moral implications. I wasn't even thinking about God. When my wife and I got married, we had no relationship with the Lord whatsoever. After a series of crises in one year, however, God got our attention. We decided to move home to the West Coast. Back home, we thought we should give our children a chance to see what religious life was about, so they could make their own decision.

The plan was to visit my old Presbyterian church, my wife Roberta's Catholic church, and then to move on to various faiths. That should have given them enough to make up their own minds about the religious stuff. Well, we didn't get past my Presbyterian church.

One morning outside the church, I began arguing with God. "I'm not sure if I want to believe in you, and I don't understand what I need to do if I become a Christian. But, I have been listening to the pastor and I am certain if I become a Christian, you will send me off to the mission field first, and that mission field will put me into ministry somewhere, probably in great poverty." I was now five years into my business career, and I had no desire to go off to the mission field. I was in business, and I really wanted to do business. I argued, "Lord, that's not what I want to do." His comment to me was, "So what? What has that got to do with your decision for me?" I finally gave in, "Whatever you decide is okay with me." His response was a verse: "Delight yourself in the Lord and he will give you the desires of your heart" (Psalm 37:4).

My desire was to be in business, so I made a request, "If you want me to be a pastor, then you will need to change the desires of my heart. I trust you, but I need you to do that for me." Not long after, I was waiting for the voice of God to again tell me where he wanted me to go. In the meantime, I was looking at ideas for possibly starting a business. A friend and I had just made a bid to buy a company and were badly beaten out of the deal. Back in my temporary office, he said he had a number of ideas for starting a business. Since I had nothing else to do that day, I encouraged him to lay them out. About halfway down the list of his business ideas, I heard a voice distinctly say, *"That's it."* Immediately I wondered who was speaking? It wasn't my friend. He was in the middle of explaining yet another business idea he had. I sensed it was God talking to me. I stopped my would-be partner and asked him to back up. Dutifully, he began to go through the list again until I said, "That one! Tell me more about that one." God began to work with us.

Our business was to provide computer users in large corporations with all they needed to run their systems. In those days there was no store for that kind of stuff. We focused on putting the concept together. Thirty years ago users bought computer accessories and supplies from the computer manufacturer. We saw an opportunity to by-pass that slow chain of purchasing and provide faster service and lower prices. We decided these sales would be too small to support a sales person, so we were going to build our computer supplies business by direct mail.

Up until then, no one had sold anything by direct mail any more complicated than a pencil, let alone rather sophisticated computer-related products. Further, direct mail was considered to be notoriously slow. It was very unusual for a direct mail company to ship everything the same day, which we were going to do. There was no Federal Express. If you ordered something via direct mail, twelve weeks was a good delivery window; eight weeks was pretty good, and six weeks was unbelievable. To get an order to the customer the next day—*nobody* did that! We had decided computer customers wanted fast service and could not wait weeks, let alone days, for a shipment to arrive.

We had little money when we started the company. Daily sales were crucial for us. Since we shipped everything the same day, we had no backlog. Daily sales grew to $1,600, then $1,700, then to over $2,000, then the company sales started to sink. With this growth, we were stretched cash-wise. I was up to my eyeballs financially and began to worry.

I talked to my wife about the sales decline and the doubts I was having about whether I should have even started the company in the first place. Perhaps I had misunderstood God's plan. Perhaps I was supposed to be a missionary after all. My wife's approach to the problem was simple: ask God to show us. Remembering that seven was the biblical number for completeness and perfection, she suggested we pray for a $7,000 day. This was way beyond our best day ever in recorded sales. In fact, it was three times our highest single day's sales, but I agreed. She went further. Since one day could be a coincidence, she believed it would be best to pray for *three* $7,000 days. I thought those numbers were nearly impossible and certainly outrageous. Not wanting to appear unspiritual, I agreed again. We decided to light a candle and keep it burning for ten days while we prayed for three $7,000 days.

We prayed morning and night. For the first five days I was really worried. How could this possibly happen? Sales continued to drift downward. On the fifth or sixth day, I began to feel that if this wasn't where God wanted me. He had something better, and I began to feel hopeful. On the tenth day, which happened to be Sunday night, I got up from the prayer time, and said, "Roberta, I really believe God's going to give us a $7,000 day." There was nothing in the numbers to give me any support, but somehow I knew what God was going to do. And she said, "You know, I feel the same way."

The next morning I went to the office and we had a little business meeting.

All four employees showed up. I said, "God is going to give us a $7,000 day today." I wish I had a photograph of the look on their faces! One person's jaw was longer than normal, eyes were larger than normal, and I could practically read their thoughts, *"Where did I put my resumé? The boss has cracked!"*

The day started like any other. Usually incoming telephone orders were constant until about 11:30 a.m., dropping off over lunch, picking up around 2:00 pm and finally tailing off at 4:30 p.m., but this day, sales started about 8:30 in the morning, which was a little unusual. Incoming orders were constant, not overwhelming Nancy, my Customer Service Rep, but very steady—one right after the other.

About 2:00 p.m., Nancy came into my office, "Ken, we could have a $5,000 day today!" She was really excited, and, in her excitement, she was going to let me off the hook. And I said, "No, it's a $7,000 day. That's what we asked for." She looked at me, shook her head, and went away.

At 5:00 p.m. the phones finally stopped ringing with the last call coming from a firm in Hawaii. In those days, as a computer company, we did not actually have a computer. So, we tabulated our daily sales using a ten-key calculator and a piece of paper. We sat there, pretty excited, while Nancy, our sales representative cum accountant, zipped away on the ten-key. She went through the numbers twice, pulled up the total, and put her fingers on the two red numbers at the bottom—$7,000!

I was absolutely over the moon, and called my wife, "Roberta, guess what?" She said, "I know, you had a $7,000 day. Now come home the kids need you." The next two Mondays, we had $7,000 days, then business dropped to $1,900 and then $1,600. But I was the happiest man in town. I didn't really care because I knew that I was right where God wanted me.

Incidentally, we found that our sales did drop only to come on stronger as the year unfolded in later months. These $7,000 days stood out in our statistics as three very unusual beacons or spikes on the daily sales chart. These spikes were never repeated although the company grew to roughly $400 million in sales per year.

Pastors are not the only serious Christians. Serious Christians are those who commit their lives to God whether in the ministry or at work. That has been my experience, and I pray that it is yours. Don't ever let people say that there is a division between us or that one person's work is nobler than another's. I defy you to find one reference in Scripture that supports the idea that God is not interested in the work of business folks or that pastors are somehow closer to God because of their clerical vocation. Work in the secular world is just as important to God as being a pastor.

DAVID MILLER on
CONNECTING FAITH and WORK

Soon after that my wife Karen, a highly successful lawyer turned law professor, and I returned to the States. I studied for several years in seminary, first for an MDiv and then a PhD in social ethics. As you've gathered by now, my passion is connecting faith and work. My personal mission statement is: How do we integrate the claims of our faith with the demands of our work? We work in a world and in a workplace that make demands on us that aren't always aligned with the claims of the Gospel. The code of ethics on Wall Street is different from the code of ethics in the Bible. How do we integrate the claims of our faith with the demands of our work?

My friend Bob Buford wrote a *New York Times* best-seller entitled, *Halftime: Changing Your Game Plan from Success to Significance.* Now theologically, what is wrong with that title? Bob made a bundle of money with cable TV in Texas. In mid-life he experienced a tragedy and some profound, life-changing events. Since then, he has dedicated the second half of his life to strategic philanthropy and a lot of other extraordinary things. He's a super guy.

His thesis in *Halftime* is once you have made your bundle, you should cash in, step out of the business world where you made your wealth and start finding significance in your life by getting involved in good works and noble projects. The problem I have with that thesis is what about the first half of your life? Does that count for nothing other than to make money for later "giving back"?

In response, one of the books I am writing has the working title of *Full Time: Finding Significance in your Success.* I believe your whole work life, whether you are an analyst, an engineer, a secretary, or a CEO, is full-time and significant. We err if we think that work can only be a calling and fulfilling if it is really stimulating, or if we work only in order to later be a philanthropist. Look at the biblical stories on calling. In most of those narratives, people were called to things that were not fun, glorious, or glamorous. They were not called to things you would aspire to do. Callings can be tough, just like the workplace. Let's embrace that and find God in the daily, the mundane, and the profane.

For example, God says to Moses, a convicted felon on the run: "I want you to pop back in and visit Pharaoh and tell him to free all the slaves." That was not a pleasant calling.

Often we start our careers working those ludicrously long hours and doing meaningless tasks, or so they seem, as we develop our professional competence. That is the place for us to be the face of Christ. That is when we are tested, learn where the ethical boundaries are, learn how to say "no," when to say "yes," and perhaps how to suffer the consequences. Those are trying times but can also be times of calling. They equip us for later things that might seem bigger or more meaningful. It is in the trenches where a lot of the learning action is.

I do a lot of one-on-one consulting, counseling, coaching, and advising with CEOs and senior executives. Many of them will start the one-on-one relationship by saying, "Aw, Miller, I really envy you. You are in full-time

Christian work." And I reply, "Do you mind if I ask you a question? Are you baptized?" Most of them are. I continue, "Well, according to what I read in the Bible, you are in full-time Christian work, too!" Being a research analyst is full-time Christian work. So is being a ditch digger, or a CEO. It is all about where we are planted, and being faithful to your call there and beyond.

Now to be fair, in some fields it is a lot harder to make the connection between work and doing what is God-pleasing and honorable. There probably are some fields that people of faith ultimately should say, "That is just too toxic, too evil, too wrong, too bad, too much against my principles. I should not work in that environment." But in general, I tend to stretch the boundary of where Christians ought to work. A Christian ought to work in as dangerous a place as possible, so long as you can protect yourself. If you don't like how certain industries operate, get in them and try to change them. Maybe you'll be there just for a season. Maybe you'll work there for just a few years. It could be very difficult for you spiritually or ethically, but maybe you will begin to create change. You can protect, empower, and encourage others. You can make a difference.

Dietrich Bonhoeffer, the Lutheran pastor, ethicist, and martyr who got involved in overthrowing Hitler, is my favorite theologian. He said, to paraphrase, "It is better to get your hands dirty in order to try to prevent evil and then to fall on the mercy of God for forgiveness then it is to sit on the sidelines and be proud of your clean hands." That motivates me.

CALLING

"WORK AS WORSHIP"

Whether you are a CEO, young entrepreneur or manager in your business, you have an enormous opportunity to give people a picture of God by the way you work.

Scan QR Code to see the Video
or go to:

http://www.rightnow.org/wawbook

CHAPTER TWO
LEADERSHIP

"The Son of Man did not come to be served, but to serve."

Matthew 20:28

Through the years, as a participant, consultant, and researcher in a variety of organizations, I have come to believe that nothing is more paramount to the success, health, and well-being of an organization than who its leaders are. It begins and ends with leadership.

For my doctoral dissertation, I researched twelve businesses and learned a lot about the interconnectedness of business organizations. The direct correlation between leadership attitudes and practices and the health of the business was astonishing. If a leader was wise and humble, then it was often reflected in the organization. If the leader was negative and arrogant, then that was found throughout the business as well.

The Bible talks a great deal about how we are to treat one another. For leaders, these teachings are magnified because leaders, by definition, are people who have influence over others. The actions of leaders affect people in ways that leaders frequently fail to recognize.

Everyone is a leader to some degree. Picking up and reading this book is an indication that you are more inclined to leadership than perhaps many others are. Whether you are a seasoned leader or an emerging one, we can all learn from one another.

In this chapter, we have the opportunity to learn from some remarkable leaders who have unique thoughts on what it means to be simultaneously a follower of Christ and a leader of people in the global marketplace.

DAVID GREEN on
RUNNING GOD'S BUSINESS

My dad was a pastor who worked in small churches. My two brothers, three sisters and I all worked picking cotton and a variety of other jobs to help the family out. It instilled in me a strong work ethic. God supplied our needs but I knew we had to work for everything we got.

My first introduction into retail was from a class I took in High School. It was called Distributive Education. I would leave school at 11:30 and go work in the local five and dime store. I discovered that I loved retail and the work. It seemed like something I could do long-term.

All five of my siblings followed my father's footsteps and went into a tradition pastoral life. After I went into retail, I thought I was a second-class Christian. Later I learned we all have a calling in our lives and God had a purpose for my life too.

Initially I was a store manager at a chain. I started to manufacture something so I could go into business myself. I began making frames in my garage. My two sons would glue frames together and my wife would ship them. We used the profits to open our first Hobby Lobby store which was very small at 300 hundred square feet.

God's Business
We always said Hobby Lobby belonged to God. It's easy to say. However, years ago we said, "What does that look like?" We've structured the business so that we have no individual rights. The rights belong to the family. We vote as a family. How we grow has to be decided as a family. We've given up person rights, stock, and ownership. This is God's business.

Legally, we have a document that says if this company is sold, no individual would gain from it. Ninety percent is to go to missions and ministries. The other ten percent would take care of our children and grandchildren, for their education, medical issues, or other needs, but not salary. We are the stewards of the business, not the owners.

The company is worth billions of dollars. What's going to happen with our children and grandchildren after we're gone? I'm confident that they would carry on as stewards but there's no assurance, this is why we have these documents.

Every day, decisions are made while thinking, "Is this what God would have us to do? Would this be pleasing to God?" We try to ask these questions.

Working on Sunday

God tests us in terms of dollars and cents. In Oklahoma City, a competitor came to compete against us and said they would bury us with their money. We were scared so we opened our stores on Sunday. We were doing $100 million on Sunday.

After a while, we felt God was leading us to close our stores on Sunday, so our employees could be with their families and go to church. We didn't know the results we would get, but we sensed it was the right thing to do We just knew we had to do what we had to do. Our banks were really concerned but we found out by closing on Sunday, we attract the better managers. The best managers care about families. Those are the people we want.

And, God has blessed us. We continue to add stores. We added 35 stores, making us 490 stores by the end of 2011 with an annual revenue of $2.5 billion dollars. God has blessed us to be a profitable company.

Employees

God has given us good employees. We do things to make it easy to work for Hobby Lobby. Our managers work a five-day week and have incentive programs. The minimum wage for all full-time employees is $12 an hour and all can grow within the company.

We have over 20,000 employees in our charge and we've hired chaplains. God wants us to take care of their financial and spiritual needs.

We want people to grow in all areas so we start them at the higher salary and only have the business opened 66 hours a week. Not many companies our size are opened only 66 hours. It helps that we close at 8:00 each night and aren't opened on Sundays. This makes us a family-friendly company.

As a result our employees take care of us. All that we do for them (insurance, wages, hours, etc.) has dramatically reduced our turnover rate and this has helped the success of the company.

Faith, Family and Business

How can one separate the secular and the sacred? I'm always discouraged when someone says that they work for a "secular business". Secular means without God. We should have God in all parts of our lives, no matter where we are. Hobby Lobby is not a secular business. We ask for God's guidance. He's part of this business. I take offense to someone saying that Hobby Lobby is a secular business.

Paul says, "Pray without ceasing" (1 Thessalonians 5:17). We ask for God's guidance and trust him to lead our paths. Do we do it every time? No, but we try to do it as much as we can. It's what we like to do and it's made a difference.

The key is to believe in God's Word. Know His way is the best way.

Many times there are things we could make extra money but we don't do it if we feel the Lord would not be pleased with it. We follow what Christ would have us do and we see miracles.

We have no long-term debt because we've followed God's will in our lives.

Family is more important than Hobby Lobby. God is first, then family, then others. What will you have gained if you have a great business and the family has not followed you? If you do what you have preached and live it, your family will follow you and that has happened in our lives.

We've had very little problems over our overt biblical values. Some have said, "This is not for me." We in no way discriminate. We feel we should have the freedom to express our views about what we believe.

Our mission field is wherever God plants us. God has purpose in our lives. If you are following God, he will have something for you no matter what occupation you choose.

DENNIS BAKKE on
THE MOST FUN WORKPLACE in HUMAN HISTORY

My great desire is to create the most fun workplace in human history.

On one of my very first trips to our first operating power plant just outside of Pittsburgh, the plant manager took me on a quick tour. On the tour I was unable to see everything in detail as I would have liked. As a result, I returned to the plant after my board meetings at a local college around 11:00 in the evening, and found myself staying until 3:00 or 4:00 in the morning talking to the staff who worked the late shift. One conversation in particular struck me deeply and forever changed how I would look at the workplace.

I was told that the people who come to work in my company at twenty-two or twenty-three years old would circle a date on the calendar thirty-five years in the future indicating when they could "get out." My workplace was like a jail sentence. It was a good workplace, but you don't circle a time thirty-five years in the future when you'll finally "get out" if you think the place is a fun place to work. It bothered me.

I talked to folks about why working at my company would feel like a jail sentence, but it wasn't till I started hearing about their life away from work that I understood. When they talked about their "outside" life, their whole demeanor changed. They loved things like bowling and golf and hunting. This gave me an idea. What is it that makes the things they were talking about fun? Take basketball, for example. What's the fun thing about playing basketball? Making a basket! When is the most fun time to make a basket? When the basket breaks the tie in the championship game. There isn't one of us who doesn't dream of ourselves in a similar situation sometime. Why is that so special? We're made in the image of God, and God wants us to use our gifts and talents to make something wonderful happen. We want to be the one to make a difference—especially when it matters most. In the workplace, decision-making is what allows us to "make something happen."

A McDonald's ad featuring Michael Jordan noted he had forty-six chances in his career to make the last tie-breaking shot. He says, "I missed more than I made." Still, he loved basketball. It's not necessarily about winning. It's about being put in the decision-making position—being responsible for a particular outcome.

The essence of humanness is that we can think, reason, make a decision, and then hold ourselves accountable for the results. When we get the chance to do that, when we get to try for the shot, even if we don't win, it's the best experience ever.

As I reflected on this discovery, it changed my entire concept of how business should work in regards to decision making. It turned my view upside down. Now, I try to limit myself to one decision a year, and let others make the majority of decisions. We require decision-makers to get advice first, but the decision is ultimately theirs.

We are made in the image of God as individuals, but are put in families and companies to work. This is the essence of a joyful workplace. It's not how much you pay or how nice you are to employees or how long their vacations are that makes a place fun. It's how much they get to walk out being made in the image of God—to what extent they are able to make decisions and take responsibility.

The Bible is gives us two great job descriptions:

1.   The Genesis stewardship mission, co-creating and co-managing with God (Genesis 1).

2.   The "Great Commission" to make disciples (Matthew 28).

I believe businesses are supposed to be part of the stewardship mission.

The purpose of business is not primarily to make money. In this modern age, God likes to use people involved in business for carrying out the great commandment to love and serve our neighbors as ourselves.

Jesus' parable of the talents is my favorite work story in the Bible (Matthew 25:14-30). The master/boss sends employees out to work.

He encourages them to take risks, make decisions, and undertake random acts of responsibility. The boss never makes any of the decisions about their work, never approves their projects. The only person who gets in trouble is the one who gets tangled up in risk management. Those that invested wisely and aggressively risked the most. It's similar to Genesis where God turns over management of the earth to Adam and to his heirs (us), and even gives away the most important decision of a person's life—to choose or reject God. In the parable of the talents, the boss ends with "Enter into the joy of your master" (Matthew 25:21, 23 ESV). There's joy in working as God meant us to.

In Kazakhstan we took over a power plant; one of the largest in the world. Our plant manager from Hawaii came with me to look at the plant. There were supposedly 5,000 people assigned to work in the power plant (although I doubt more than 3,000 ever worked there). I tried to get them to understand that we were about letting people make decisions. There was absolutely no response, just blank stares. They could not relate. They were not used to acting or being treated like people.

So, I left my Hawaiian manager there to lead the people and went back every summer. On my last trip there, three years later, I asked them to tell me stories. They told how their lives had been changed. They were able to make decisions, things happened, and sometimes things didn't work out, but they had a purpose for living. At the end of the session there was a five- to ten-minute standing ovation—a celebration of pure joy.

It is not optional to give people freedom to make decisions, nor is it optional for leaders who are followers of Christ to refrain from making decisions. It is necessary for the fulfillment of the stewardship commission.

Labor and *opus* are two Latin words for "work." *Labor* conjures up a picture of something hard and difficult. *Opus* denotes something creative and wonderful. When you do the *work* God has called you to do, do it with a passion, joy, and the love befitting God's call on your life.

HOWARD DAHL on THE CALL OF LEADERSHIP

Being a leader begins with seeing yourself as called to a position of leadership and therefore to service. "If you want to be great, you must be the servant of all the others " (Matthew 20:26 CEV). A lot of us want to be called a servant, but we don't want to be treated as one. It can be difficult to have humility about your call and your role when you've had success and lots of positive feedback. Part of the call of leadership is to take the well-being of all of your employees seriously—to see your position as a steward charged to care for your employees.

DAVID MORKEN on FOLLOWING CHRIST'S EXAMPLE OF LEADERSHIP

Most of our 170 employees work in our three-story building in Cary, North Carolina. It's hugely humbling to lead such a large and talented team. Christ's life demonstrates principles that inform leadership every hour and every minute, and his example of leadership begins with serving.

I'm not deceived about myself. I know I am very mortal and can make many, many mistakes. To be in a position to hire someone is humbling and to be in a position to fire them is also humbling. Christ's example of humility is mind-blowing. He was the greatest man to ever walk the planet and was a servant, washing the feet of others, giving his life, taking on sin he didn't deserve. With him as my Savior, it's incumbent upon me to make sure I don't have an elitist approach to leadership. There is great value in hierarchy, chain of command, and authority; without those, people usually do not accomplish what they're most capable of accomplishing. However, how you handle authority and how you treat people is key. You can easily crush somebody's spirit by demeaning them, not believing in them, exalting yourself and taking credit for their work, or, even worse, by trying to do *their* job from a position above them. Keeping Christ's example in mind reminds me I am here to serve.

DENNIS BAKKE on
INFLUENCING LEADERS

If you are not a leader now, you are likely going to be a leader someday. Understanding the role of leadership now prepares you for the future. You also have a chance to teach those leading with you the biblical way to lead.

Warning: You may get fired. I was at the World Bank teaching about changing the way we do things. Located in Washington, DC, the World Bank is involved in microfinance and other financial assistance around the globe. About 10,000 people work for the bank and 8,000 are housed in Washington. A young woman, a middle manager for Bolivia, asked how she could implement the changes I was suggesting. I told her, "You can do all of these things, but you and the people who work for you need to move to Bolivia. Give your people the freedom to make decisions after getting advice from you and their colleagues. You will have to protect your people from the bosses above you. Also you're probably going to lose your job. If you're not prepared to lose your job, you probably won't have the courage to make the changes."

She responded by moving her team to Bolivia and creating a successful team. It was hard work and she had to run interference with her bosses to let her people make decisions. You have to free your subordinates to make decisions, but you also have to protect them from senior management who don't see the importance of this kind of empowerment. It's difficult, but not impossible, to do your part as a leader from a "lower" position.

JOHN TYSON on
FAITH IN LEADERSHIP

Faith helps me tremendously in the marketplace. In day-to-day business problems, it helps me see the impact I have on the individuals I'm dealing with. Also my faith enables me to let things go.

In leadership positions, we get on a treadmill, and every time we think we are in shape, they turn the treadmill up again. My faith allows me to slow down and realize the broader issue. One day, they'll turn that treadmill off, and if we don't have our faith in place, we're going to fall flat on our face and be lost. We will have been chasing the treadmill of life—the next bonus, the next job promotion, or whatever—and find ourselves asking, "What do I do now?" because we've missed something essential.

Most of all, my faith allows me to step back and acknowledge that all of us are just trying to get up and get along every day—to make a difference and find the right answers. Some days are better than others, but, in the end, we're striving to honor God. We'll get it eighty percent right. We'll never get one hundred percent right one hundred percent of the time, but eighty percent is not bad in the business world.

STEVE REINEMUND on
LEADERS SHARING FAITH in THE WORKPLACE

The higher we go in an organization, particularly in a publicly held company, the more sensitive we must be to not create a situation or the perception that in order to advance one must embody the same beliefs as the leadership. Some may disagree with this perspective, and I respect that, but personally, I am careful how overtly I express my faith. I do not want people to feel they can't succeed if they believe differently than I do. They must embrace the same general values and ethics, but their path to acquiring these can be very different.

I have not taken an active role in trying to evangelize, especially in the workplace. The success of leaders is based on their principles. You can derive those principles in many ways. For me, they come through my faith, but I respect however you arrive at those principles as long as you have the same high ethical standards as the company. And I leave it at that. In public and even in private companies, leaders have to be sensitive to not project their faith onto others.

2

LEADERSHIP

"MORE THAN A HOBBY"

How can you worship God through your work? In this interview, CEO and Founder of Hobby Lobby, David Green, discusses how he uses the talents and resources God gave him in business to enlarge God's kingdom and to serve his employees and customers.

Scan QR Code to see the Video
or go to:

http://www.rightnow.org/wawbook

CHAPTER THREE
CHARACTER

"May your whole spirit, soul and body be kept blameless at the coming of our Lord Jesus Christ."

1 Thessalonians 5:23b

Followers of Christ generally understand that we are called to live according to his teachings and example. Yet it is frequently difficult to know how that translates into our work lives in ways other than, say, "Don't lie, cheat, or steal." We know there are a few things we should not do. So we avoid those, do our work, and go our merry way.

However, character is a much deeper issue than simply avoiding a few obvious wrongs. It is also about what we do and how we live. Our character is, perhaps, most clearly revealed when times are the toughest. Many businesses are going through very tough times financially right now; some are even collapsing. As a result, our collective character is being challenged. How we handle the trying circumstances of our lives shapes and forms who we are.

Character is exposed in both the best of times and the worst of times. It can be seen in how we treat others. Character is who we are at our core. As people of faith in the global marketplace, we are called to live as Christ, regardless of our situation. This means to conduct ourselves with integrity in times of adversity, to treat people with kindness and respect, and a host of other things that are easier said than done.

Life at work is not as it is at church where we can get by with smiling, greeting one another, and saying we're fine. In the workplace we spend endless hours with one another trying to work out difficult situations, and as pressures mount, both our good and bad sides are revealed. In this chapter, we learn from leaders who have developed strong character through a variety of life circumstances.

HOWARD DAHL on
INTEGRITY

Integrity includes never asking any employee to do something that compromises his or her own ethics. For example, never ask a salesman to exaggerate or to deceive in any way to get a sale. Never allow yourself or employees to speak ill of competitors.

There was a time in our company's history when we got into deep financial difficulty. Our bank called in our line of credit and we owed two hundred thirty people money. Our bank wanted us to go into bankruptcy. It was November 20, 1987, almost at the end of the farm crisis of the 1980s. I prayed and fasted for about sixty hours, and out of that came a letter that I wrote to all 230 of our suppliers.

In thinking through what to do, the clarity that I discovered was unbelievable. How would I want to be treated if I were owed money? The answer was that I would want the truth, the whole truth. So I wrote a letter spelling out all the ugly details of where we were financially.

Over the next two years, I communicated with our creditors through a series of letters and personally took the accounts payable calls. I didn't want any of our employees to receive abuse from people to whom we owed money. After two years, we were able to work through it and pay them all back. We received incredible feedback from those people we had owed money to. There was only one company out of 230 that moved against us and tried to sue us to force collection. The rest were gracious and thanked me for being straightforward with them.

Some of the very best times of spiritual growth and spiritual dependency came through the most difficult days of our businesses. When you go through difficulties, how you respond is a real test. Do you have a tendency to take shortcuts in either good times or bad, or do you have an ever-present sense of what God would have you do in every situation? These can be tremendous times of character shaping.

During the difficult days for Concord in the late 1980s, we would often not know at the beginning of the week how we would meet pay-roll on Friday. For three years God provided manna--just enough with no excess--and we never missed a payroll. This was an intense time of learning about God's power and faithfulness.

The uncertainty of business also leads us to dependency on God. There's no real presumption in business. This particular lesson is hitting home hard right now. You can have seven years of solid growth and instantly be thrown into a challenging situation where many customers can't get credit. You can never presume you know the future. It drives us to depend on God.

STEVE LYNN on
GROWTH THROUGH CHALLENGES

You will find, or already know, there is something different about life's hurts when they relate to your children. I think back to the most devas-tating news of my life. I have a vivid recollection of my wife's call from the doctor's office to tell me that our four-year-old son had permanently lost fifty percent of his hearing through a bad case of the chicken pox. He would wear hearing aids for the rest of his life. I couldn't believe it. The absolute weight of the world was on my shoulders; however the promise I learned earlier still spoke to me. This unconditional promise that "in all things God works for the good of those who love him" (Ro-mans 8:28) says there is a light at the end of the tunnel; there is an end to the pain; there is always hope. Call it faith if you want. The human spirit can overcome and endure unbelievable things if there is hope.

I wish it were not true, but there will be terrible, awful, very bad days in your personal and professional life. How you respond to them will determine your success in life. You will not be all that you were made to be unless there is something in your spirit that gives you hope. We must have a different view of success. We tend to put successful leaders on a pedestal and say, "They don't get scared like I do. They don't mess up like I do. They don't have morning breath like I do."

That is simply not true. To think otherwise would be to believe that Michael Jordan could do all those wonderful things with a basketball the first time he picked it up. Every great athlete who has ever lived has experienced miserable failure at some point, but what made that person great is having never given up. Likewise, the only successful leaders were at one time miserable failures who simply never gave up. Failure is just an unpleasant good—it is how we learn to search for and find success. We must think of success as the process of failing forward.

NORM MILLER on
REAL BUSINESS

In 1978, I purchased control of a battery company from its founder (Interstate Batteries). My brother, who was also in the business, became a follower of Christ within 6 months. When I took over the company, there were other Christians in the business. We had important discussions. How could we lift up Christ in business? We could lose employees, be sued. We might lose customers and all of the business. How far were we willing to go?

We had to think this out. We prayed about it. I thought of Matthew 10:28, "Do not be afraid of those who kill the body but cannot kill the soul. Rather, be afraid of the One who can destroy both soul and body in hell.

My brother, Tommy, and I decided, "Ok, God, we're going to do everything you want us to do. We don't want to offend anyone. We want to honor You."

We would be alert and bold. We asked God for perfect boldness and perfect sensitivity. That's how we started out. We had a saying. If we pay, we pray. If we took people to dinner, we would have a prayer before dinner or we would pray before meetings with our colleagues. Thank God we haven't been sued.

The Golden Rule at Work

My work with Interstate Batteries is a business—selling batteries. It's fun to sell more. I like to sell more batteries. We also have a platform. Through discipleship, we try to walk with God and honor him 24/7. How do we do this in the business?

Our mission statement is "treat people the way you want to be treated." It's in our statement. Even our distributors, independent business people say, "I feel that this is God's commandment." If you don't, that's ok. I'm not going to tell you how to think. We just think this is the best way to do business.

You can tell when someone has your interest at heart. We want to treat people the way we want to be treated. If we make them happy, they'll come back. Then, we move on to the next guy and make the business grow. We set upon excellence. If we hang God's name on this thing, we want to be number one. We've sold more batteries in the US every year for the last 20 years. We sold 17.4 million batteries last year.

Beyond Money

Our competitor started having national conventions. So we decided we needed to do a convention and our first in Hawaii in 1982. Before the convention, I had some concerns. We're getting all of these people together, but what are we doing?

We prayed and made a list of everything we wanted out of this convention. We wanted some business, but we wanted there to be love. We made a prayer list everyday for the convention.

When we went to Hawaii, we had people praying for us. Everyone truly loved each other. Then I realized we should pray every day about everything. We made another list and started praying. We would dedicate ten minutes or so a day, then get on to business. I would be late with a laundry list of to do's but I would always force myself to pray. If you're a soldier and you were going into battle, you would just do it. I had to view prayer as the same for us.

Eventually, we decided to have conventions on the weekend so we could have a Sunday morning service. We included buffet and lunch and we would say, "It's Sunday morning, so let's have a service. We brought people in like, Tom Landry and Michael W. Smith. We had nice meals and music and we had testimony. We've been doing it since 1984.

CHARACTER
"CREATED TO CREATE"

▼

In this real-life story, Megan shares how her career as a designer for Ralph Lauren in New York City is really her mission field. Both in the way she reflects the character of the Infinite Creator through exceptional design, and how she can love and care for her co-workers for the glory of Christ.

Scan QR Code to see the Video
or go to:

http://www.rightnow.org/wawbook

CHAPTER FOUR
SUCCESS

"O LORD, God of my master Abraham, if you will, please grant success to the journey on which I have come."

Genesis 24:42

Success is probably one of the most loaded words in the English language, particularly as it relates to the intersection of faith and work. In the business world, success is generally defined in terms of money and power, and little else. In the sports world, success is defined as winning. But does that translate to life? Winning at what?

Ralph Waldo Emerson reportedly said, "The line between failure and success is so fine that we scarcely know when we pass it—so fine that we often are on the line and do not know it." Success is something we strive for but cannot define well. What is success? If you took sixty seconds right now, could you formulate a sentence or two about what you think success is?

Should followers of Christ seek to be successful in the eyes of the "world"? Or is success something we should view negatively? What does success look like from a divine and biblical perspective?

Defining success is of utmost importance because it is what guides our goals, our processes, and ultimately our actions. Intuitively rejecting or accepting conventional wisdom about success is insufficient. We need to meditate on success, pray about it, discuss it with others, come to some real decisions, and then live in accordance to that definition.

MO ANDERSON on KELLER WILLIAMS REALTY: VALUES THAT FEED THE SOUL and FUEL GROWTH

People frequently ask how Keller Williams Realty has built the kind of business culture that values God and family first, and then, secondarily, business. The short answer would be that the journey began with leadership who are very grounded in their personal and business values and have never been afraid to state what those values are.

When I joined Keller Williams Realty back in 1992, I was very certain about what I believed in and what I stood for. I had some major opportunities with big-name companies, but I turned them down because their values were not compatible with mine.

I thank God that I said no, because two years later, I discovered a tiny real estate company with five hundred agents in seven offices that were able to clearly articulate their values. These values, called the "WI4C2TS," serve as nine covenant agreements that guide how they do business as a company and how they treat each other.

Nearly twenty years later, I have no doubt this little company was where I was called to be. I felt that this would be Jesus' way of running a company, and I knew in my heart that we were absolutely a match.

The Keller Williams Realty W-I-4C-2T-S

Win-Win or no deal

Integrity do the right thing

Customers always come first

Creativity ideas before results

Commitment in all things

Communication seek first to understand

Trust starts with honesty

Teamwork together everyone achieves more

Success results through people

I believed it so strongly that I was willing to forego a salary and embraced the entrepreneurial experience that was before me. This was truly a leap of faith because, at the time, my husband and I were totally broke. The recession of the late 1980s had left us penniless.

So I turned to two of my friends, John and Paul, and asked them to loan us money. (Aren't those interesting names?) They loaned the money for one reason. They trusted my values. And so, in 1992, I opened the first region of this fledgling company that was outside of Texas.

Three years later, in 1995, having experienced a high degree of success establishing Keller Williams Realty within Oklahoma, I was asked by Gary Keller, the company's co-founder, to step up to the role of CEO and president.

I had no idea what a CEO did, so I turned him down. Gary persisted in asking me to consider this opportunity and my husband encouraged me as well. So I finally said "yes" on the condition that I could have a really low salary and a sizeable percentage of ownership in the company.

What followed was a tremendous growth journey as Keller Williams Realty grew to become the third largest real estate company in the United States, with more than 70,000 associates and close to 700 market centers throughout North America. Having replaced myself as CEO in 2005, and stepping into the role of Vice Chairman of Keller Williams Realty and Chairman of KW Cares, it has given me great joy to observe that the WI4C2TS principles are as widely celebrated throughout our company as they have ever been.

There's no question that we have stumbled along the way, but I believe that what has strengthened our company and powered us forward is an unyielding belief in what we stand for, as well as well-defined systems and standards that provide a framework for growth.

Looking back over the past two decades, here's what I observe to be the key factors that have driven our company and our culture.

A determination to get into business with people who share our common values

That is easier said than done, but as I once heard Ken Blanchard, author of many best-selling books, observe, "If you build a company with your values, then similar people with similar values will be attracted to it."

In addition to the WI4C2TS, our Keller Williams values are:

1. God and family first and the business second.
2. Our associates should be treated like stakeholders.
3. A stakeholder company should measure profit or loss, should open the books, and should tell the truth.
4. Profit matters. And if we're profitable, we have an obligation to share that profit with the people who helped make the profit.
5. Who we are in business with really matters.
6. No transaction is worth our reputation.

As a result of holding these values, I've had to make a lot of tough choices. When I first started my journey as president and CEO in 1995, I quickly discovered that Keller Williams Realty had gotten into business with a lot of people who did not share our values. So I began a very difficult two-year process of getting our company on the right track. There were 1,800 agents and forty offices at the time. I closed fifteen offices and got out of business with seventeen managers. It was hard, and it nearly killed my happy, fun-loving spirit.

We then set about the mission of positioning the company for growth, and that's exactly what we got. In 2002, Keller Williams Realty became the nation's seventh largest real estate company; in 2003, we were the sixth largest; the following year, we moved into the top five; in 2006 we gained Prudential's spot as number four; and in 2009 we replaced RE/MAX as the third largest real estate company in the United States. I have no doubt that we are destined to become number one.

An unapologetic statement of values and belief

Every month, I conduct a seminar for approximately two hundred prospective franchise owners, market center leaders, market center investors, and agents. I teach them how our models work, and I teach them how to launch a new market center. We call this Franchise Systems Orientation—formerly known as Launch Boot Camp.

I review our mission statement: Careers worth having—Businesses worth owning—Lives worth living. I point out that a career worth having requires profit, a business worth owning requires profit, and a life worth living will mean something different to all of us. Then I move into sharing our values, but before I begin, I let all prospective franchisees know before they consider getting into business with us that the leaders of this company are followers of Christ. And then I make a long pause. I emphasize that we are very, very proud of our diversity. If you were to ask our Muslim, Buddhist, Hindu, or Jewish agents if they feel loved and supported in our company and our culture, they would tell you "yes."

Once, two men asked for my assistance to help them negotiate a settlement for the breakup of their business. I will never forget that meeting. One of the men was Jewish. The other was Christian. I looked at both of them and said, "You worship the God of Abraham; you are a Christian. You worship the God of Abraham; you are Jewish. I want us to take each others' hands and begin this meeting in prayer." I prayed that God would give us wisdom. I prayed that God would give them the courage to tell the truth to each other, and I prayed most of all that the friendship would be restored. It was a friendship that had begun the first day of college. God honored that prayer because those two later shared with me that they had reconciled.

I understand clearly that bringing the name of God into our business dealings is not politically correct, and I don't care. In twelve years, I have had only one person walk out highly offended that the name God or Christ had been spoken in a business seminar.

An emphasis on wealth building and stewardship

During Franchise Systems Orientation, I emphasize to all attendees that they need to be excited about building wealth, and if they are not excited about becoming wealthy, we are not a match. I point out that it is not about the money; it is about what the money can do.

I explain that we should never be afraid to pray and ask God to let us know whether we are meant to be wealthy, because it is all his and we are only the guardians for a short period of time. Once wealth comes to us, it is our obligation to ensure that we have the training and the knowledge to make sure that money is spent wisely and given away wisely.

I grew up in total poverty as the daughter of an Oklahoma sharecropper in the 1930s and 1940s. My family did not have any money, and today, there is no greater joy for me than the joy of writing out a check to someone who needs help.

Incorporate value and standards into company literature, legal documents, and training classes

Our values are repeated over and over. The leaders of our company have signature cultural stories that stand as classic demonstrations of the specific values that mean so much to our company. When a person in one of our departments comes to one of our managers and shares a moral dilemma, they are able to refer back to a story or a decision that has determined who we are as a company.

Call your people to a higher standard

Whenever I visit one of our company's regions or offices, I ask for stories that support the values that we espouse as a company.

I visited a North Carolina office several years ago and one of the agents said, "Mo, we have a great story. Joe took a listing on a property, and then proceeded to purchase it. The next day, another agent, who hadn't checked the computer to see that the property was already listed as sold, made an offer for far more money. Joe walked into his team leader's office and said, 'I have a dilemma. What do I do? If I were with my old company, I would have simply told the other agent that the property had sold, because that is all I am legally required to do, but I'm with Keller Williams now, and the WI4C2TS calls me to a higher standard.'"

Joe was exactly right. Based on the guidance from his team leader, he took the higher offer to the seller and rescinded his offer for the benefit of his client. A values-based culture changes people's behavior. Miraculously, profits and growth have followed. In fact, Keller Williams Realty has outpaced the real estate industry every step along the way. Within a matter of ten years, we grew from 2,000 agents to more than 70,000.

In 2009, during one of the most challenging real estate markets and worst economic downturns in history, we shared more than $32 million in profits with our associates. Since 1997, we've given more than $270 million back to our people in the form of profit share. Sharing market center profits with the people who have helped to make them has extended the light, love, and the opportunity of our company. I believe that our culture is at the heart of our company's phenomenal growth. It is who we are. And the growth is exciting because the sky's the limit.

There's a hunger in the hearts and minds of most of the people in this country to be affiliated with an organization that has integrity and cares about more than just profit. More people come to our company because of the culture—the regard we have for each other, our families, and our spiritual beliefs—than for any other reason.

Giving, sharing, and helping is just who we are. It's in our hearts; it's in our minds; it's at our core. Each of us is growing along with the growth of Keller Williams Realty, and together, we stand as a constellation of success.

I often find myself wondering how in the world an Oklahoma farm girl ended up as vice chairman of the third largest real estate company in the United States. I'll never fully be able to answer that question, but I do know that God has a plan for all of our lives that is greater than anything we could imagine. A lesson that I've learned over and over again in my life is that "all things work together for good, for those who are called according to his purpose" (Romans 8:28), and that there is always a spiritual lesson in adversity. My husband and I were in our 50s in the 1980s when we lost everything and had to start over again. I now realize that losing all our money was the greatest thing that ever happened to us, because it sparked the chain of events that led us to Keller Williams Realty.

BRIAN LEWIS on
SUCCESS AND FAILURE

What is perhaps least understood about success is that many successful people are burdened by it. They see what they have accomplished, but it feels small compared to what they hoped might have been possible. The story is the same, whether it is the councilman who becomes a state senator but is never elected to Congress; the president elected with great fanfare but leaves office with the ambitions of his first years largely unfulfilled; the best-selling author who achieves financial acclaim, but her work is never taken seriously for its literary merit; or the esteemed scientist, who never holds the Nobel Prize.

Once I worked with a CEO who had made a long journey from a modest beginning. He was now leading a nearly $200 million a year global company. Yet, in his quiet moments, he would tell me, "My friends from business school now lead billion-dollar firms. They run publicly-traded companies."

Success has its satisfactions, but also its own set of burdens.

This is why success should always be held lightly, for it is squirrelly. Winning has a way of producing a temporary euphoria that recedes quickly and routinely, like the tide. This is why *defining* success—understanding what we personally mean by this word—is one of the most important tasks of our lives. It can be a waste to run hard for a goal that you discover was never what you hoped it would be. Ideally, we should clearly define "success" for ourselves at the outset of our careers, but this rarely occurs. Typically, we define success as we live life on the run.

Developing a thoughtful understanding of failure is just as important as defining success. Failure is often calibrated to the scale of our ambitions. Fear of failure can cause ambitions to be miniaturized. If someone's ambitions are audacious, there will be a certain inevitability of failure.

One of the great pities is when superior talent is joined with inferior ambitions. This is why each of us should experience some measure of failure. If we never fail, perhaps it is because our ambitions have been miniaturized. Perhaps unbroken success should rouse our suspicions.

Leaders of philanthropic organizations in particular should respect the way in which success and failure is calibrated to outsized or miniaturized ambitions. For many years, I have worked with HOPE International (HI) on its board of trustees. HI is a Christian organization seeking to "invest in the dreams of the poor" through micro-enterprise loans. In its mission statement, HI says that it intends to "work in the hard places of the world"—to pick the places where the obstacles are greatest, the governments most unstable, and where people have experienced the most chronic disappointment. What you can expect from an organization that works in the easy places is perhaps different from what you can expect from an organization that chooses life in the hard places. Failure, as much as success, should be measured in conjunction with levels of ambition.

Indeed, a thoughtful approach to failure is an intrinsic part of "good process." For many years I have worked with Scandinavian companies, and during weekends in Stockholm often visited the old town section called *Gamla stan*. On the cobblestone streets of this historic district is a handsome building housing the Nobel Museum, which celebrates the winners of the Nobel Prize.

The Nobel Museum chronicles how great leaps forward in science typically occur. Progress is almost always an intermittent process—one step forward is followed by two steps backward, and then another step forward. The Nobel landscape is the story of how scientists and artists who take journeys worth taking use failure.

Great discoverers *study* failure to understand why dead ends are dead ends, why some doors close and other doors open. Great discoverers expect failure and never fear it. Failure is not denied or disguised; rather, failure is analyzed and followed to see where it might lead, to learn what secrets it has to reveal.

As Christians, we know failure is often not what it seems. What seemed to be the day of greatest failure—the crucifixion of Jesus—was not the end of the story. The great discovery—the resurrection of Jesus—lay just around the corner. This is in part why Christians should be among those most comfortable with acknowledging reality. There should be less need for pretending in us. Yet sometimes, even with Christian leaders, fear of failure leads to a bending of reality, and the distortions of a bad process.

Many years ago, a publicly-traded company hired me to evaluate their prospective new marketing campaign. The CEO had built a large enterprise and was a person of faith, yet he had created a culture that suffered from candor-deficit disorder. After I entered the boardroom and offered my thoughts to the CEO and his team, I watched as the team waited, waited—and then waited some more—for the CEO to speak, so they could calibrate their views to his. This was a company culture that would eventually stumble, because when candor is an at-risk behavior, the mistakes of groupthink often follow. A culture that disguises failure is always at greater risk than a culture that looks for its lessons. One of our goals should be an inner freedom that allows us to be the most-candid, most honest people in the room in our respective organizations.

In contrast, some company cultures use failure as a competitive strength. One of the leaders of a Swedish client has often said failure is his company's great moment of opportunity. It is when a product fails, my colleague says, that a customer learns the truth about the culture of their suppliers. In the case of my Swedish client, failure is the moment of truth when customers see whether marketing language about "never walking away from a problem" is true in real life. This company's most abiding customer relationships have always resulted from failures.

Many of the great turning-point decisions in our lives will be shaped by how we understand these ideas of success and failure. As Christians, we are told we must build our lives on rock, not sand, yet recognizing which is which in "real time" is not always easy. What is the sand, and what is the rock? Those of us in mid-career or late-career may have the luxury of re-balancing our lives to bring them into better alignment, but young people entering demanding careers—law, medicine, business—tend to inevitably find themselves in the eye of the storm. Significant achievement in these careers can require a focus of time and attention that is inherently unbalancing.

What then can we hope for? We can expect to at times make poor decisions, but we can learn to not get stuck. We can expect that our definitions of success will be tested, and perhaps changed. We can expect to fail, but we can learn to fail well, because our ambitions are properly proportioned. We can strive for the inner freedom that will allow us to be some of the most honest, most candid people in the room.

TYLER SELF on
TWO ESSENTIAL QUALITIES FOR SUCCESS

If you were given the opportunity to be endowed with two qualities critical to business success, which would you choose? Would you prefer the super-intelligence of a Nobel scholar combined with a handsome face? Perhaps the credibility of a world leader combined with uncanny sales and marketing acumen? What must one have to establish a successful company that thrives over the long term?

In 1946, at a small restaurant outside of Atlanta, Truett Cathy and his brother, Ben, sat exhausted one Saturday evening after covering six twenty-four-hour shifts between the two of them. The founder of Chick-fil-A® decided to close the restaurant the next day, and over the sixty-three years since, every Chick-fil-A® restaurant has closed its doors on Sunday.

Some doubt that any restaurant could survive without the most important sales day of the week, and some have marveled that Chick-fil-A® could thrive in spite of the lost day, yet Truett Cathy asserts that the business has grown because of that decision. He reminds others of the fourth commandment: to work six days and reserve the seventh for rest. His decision may be the one thing that has set the company apart. God honored Mr. Cathy for his obedience in this area and many other areas of his life.

I was privileged to spend an afternoon with Mr. Cathy a few years ago, and it became clear to me that he possessed two essential ingredients for success. You will find these two qualities in any successful investor.

The first is wisdom: the wisdom to know what to do and what to avoid. The second is confidence: the confidence to take action on wisdom. Mr. Cathy had the wisdom to close his restaurants on Sunday, but more importantly, he had the confidence to step out in faith and lock the doors.

The most substantial investor in my business is a highly revered money manager in Texas. He spoke to me a few years ago of one of his investments in a small private company in California. The company is now very large and very well known, and his original risk was extremely profitable. What did it take to multiply the investment many times over? It took the wisdom to know that the opportunity was a good investment and the confidence to take hard-earned money and entrust it to the company's founders, nothing more. He has applied this simple formula over and over with extraordinary success.

The amazing revelation about wisdom and confidence is, as children of God, we have unlimited access to both through our relationship with Christ. In James 1:5, the Lord promises to give his perfect wisdom to whoever asks of it by faith. David said in Psalm 27 that he found his confidence in the Lord.

As a young entrepreneur, I recognize that my wisdom is relatively low on the scale; thus, I must pray daily in faith for wisdom. Others may find that confidence wanes as the years pass, and they must pray daily for confidence. Solomon chose wisdom and became famous among the kings and queens of his day, and he has remained known for his wisdom ever since. If we ask the Father through faith, he will freely and generously pour out both wisdom and confidence.

HENRY KAESTNER on
DOING THE RIGHT THING

As David Morken and I were starting Bandwidth.com, we were more than eager for business clients to buy Internet access from us. In January 2001, we shifted our model from lead referral—where we sent interested businesses directly to carriers—to one of agency—where we transacted the business directly with customers—and we weren't sure it would work. To make matters worse, 2001 was quite possibly the worst time in recent history to raise money from outside investors. The Internet bubble had just burst and telecommunications companies had fallen out of favor. Imagine a new start up that was a telecom dotcom! It took us three and a half months to get our first customer and times were lean. We were eager for leads. We were eager for customers, and we were desperate to make payroll. One type of buyer came to us over and over again, ready, willing, and able to buy large quantities of Internet access from us with the cash to make it happen. One of the largest consumers of bandwidth was—and still is—the adult entertainment industry.

This sector and its ready cash loomed above us like a Jezebel with the promise of relief from our short-term cash woes. We made a firm decision not to call back any leads of suspicious origin and made our policy clear to our sales representatives. Several times after celebrating wins with our team, we unilaterally cancelled the deal because we found the buyer we thought was legitimate was a front for a pornography business. Those losses were very hard; however, David and I were resolute in our decision that, no matter how much we needed cash, we would never, ever do anything to assist an industry responsible for tearing apart so many lives and families.

Through God's grace and providence, Bandwidth.com was able to get through that perilous time and become the fastest growing telecom company over the last five years, and the fourth fastest growing privately held company of any kind. David and I are not perfect stewards of the gifts God has given us and have made many mistakes along the way; we are indeed fallen men in a fallen world. But we have committed our lives and our business to God and try to be as faithful as we can possibly be. We believe our reliance on Him, especially through the challenging times in the early days of the company is the reason for our success. We pray he will continue to give us the strength to be good and faithful servants and to use our success for his glory.

STEVE LYNN on
A SUCCESSFUL JOURNEY

I grew up on the proverbial other side of the tracks in a little southwestern Georgia cotton-mill town. For as far back as I can remember I wanted to get to the other side, to the kind of housing I saw there, to air conditioning, good food, and cleanliness. I have also always wanted to be the CEO of a company. Not because I understood exactly what that meant; rather, because the owners and leaders of companies in my hometown took an interest in me, and I wanted to be like them.

I have always been very driven. I went to college on an athletic scholarship, graduated with an engineering degree, did my MBA at the University of Louisville, and began my career. At twenty-nine, I became president of a company and married my wife, Milah. I had achieved a major life goal and had some of what the great American dream is all about: a nice California house, pool, wife, sheepdog, and Mercedes. But I was respectfully ignoring my new trophy wife—she wasn't a full partner in my life. Being president of the company was all that mattered.

Then one day, life, in the form of Milah, grabbed me by the shoulders, shook me, and caused me to slow down long enough to focus on my priorities. Standing in the foyer of that California house, she asked me, "What are the most important things in your life?" I responded, "Power, recognition, and money." A look of pain crossed her face. I'm a salesman by nature and fast on my feet, so I added, "Darling, it goes without saying that you're number one." But she knew the truth.

We lived an hour and a half away from my work. There is something therapeutic about long drive times; they give you time to reflect. So I started thinking about life, my priorities, and our wedding vows on my next trip to the office. I realized our vows meant absolutely nothing to me. I just repeated what the pastor said without thinking about them. I hadn't made a genuine commitment.

A few months later, driving to work, I made an unconditional commitment that I was going to spend the rest of my life with Milah—a choice that simplified and changed everything. For example, externally, I am a low-key, laid-back, southern gentleman, but internally, I am a hard-driving competitor. When we had disagreements, I won them all; that was my nature. I endured until she gave up. But if I wanted to spend the rest of my life with this lady, that wouldn't work. There had to be a win-win partnership.

Physical beauty was important to me, and she was and is beautiful. But God, time, and gravity take care of this physical beauty for us all. How would I happily grow old with her? I refocused my view on what attracts me to her, so, like a great bottle of wine, she only got better with age. This unconditional commitment was a major step for a self-centered, ambitious, ex-athlete like myself. It was the first time in my life I made a commitment to anything or anyone that didn't focus on "What's in it for me?"

Growing up I never went to church. When Milah and I began irregularly attending a large Presbyterian church near our home, I didn't know the rules. I didn't know when to stand up or sit down; whether to sing all four verses or just the first and third. It was boring. But we started going to a large class of young married couples like us. A tall basketball-type guy from the class began to visit me. He was on staff with Campus Crusade. I could play basketball with him, elbow him, try to beat him, and discovered Christians weren't pushovers. This was a new revelation for me.

I decided to prove to him and me that God didn't exist. We met for a whole year about this; he was very loving and patient. I would ask questions like, "How could a God of love let my friend's mother suffer with cancer for three years before she died?" As the year wore on, I didn't get all of my questions answered, but somehow they got less important. At the same time, through my father-in-law, a Christian businessman, I was discovering you could be successful and still love the Lord—also a new revelation for me.

Once again, driving to work, I had a change of heart and said a simple, naïve, inadequate prayer and turned my life over to Jesus. There were no voices. I didn't feel any different. But as the days, weeks, and months went by, my life changed from the inside out. My marriage was healed and blessed, work became less important, and I felt like I did a better job at it.

However, when Jesus captures our hearts, the promise isn't that it will all be easy. The promise is that we belong to him, and he'll be there whatever comes. Two months later, my company's parent sold and a representative of the new owners called me into his office. An hour and a half later, I left his office remembering only two words, "You're fired." At twenty-nine, I had achieved my life's major goal, and at thirty-two, it felt like it was ripped away from me.

While I was out of work for several months, I experienced the bruised ego, frustration, self-doubt, confusion, and anger that anyone goes through when they lose something precious. Two weeks after being fired, my brother-in-law called to tell me that my father had shot and killed himself. One of the men who had been instrumental in leading me to this newfound faith, called to share his condolences. He shared Romans 8:28 (NKJV), "We know that all things work together for good to those who love God." It did not make me feel any better. But, as the days went by, and I combined my new faith with this unconditional promise, I came to believe that no matter what I went through, there was hope. For over thirty years now, this verse has helped me through the "bumps in the road" that life deals us all.

I became reemployed as COO for a Los Angeles-based restaurant chain. During this time, Milah and I went to Campus Crusade for Christ headquarters for a one-week training session for business executives and their spouses. One of Sonic's largest franchisees and his wife were attending and we became friends. Upon returning home, he recommended me to Sonic's founder, Troy Smith. When he retired, I was brought in to take his place.

A different view of success

The company was in a state of decline. Sales had dipped below $200 million. Sonic was a publicly-traded company with a market value of $5 million. The company had closed over four hundred stores in the four years before I arrived, as well as experiencing four straight years of same store sales decline. None of our 930 stores in eighteen states advertised or purchased together. It was an old, weary, fifties-style carhop business with lots of deferred maintenance. Average annual store sales were only $210,000. We owned and operated 110 stores that were losing $1.5 million a year.

We had an old, out-dated license agreement with our franchisees. The agreement had no required advertising fund and collected the royalty as a fixed mark-up on our paper goods. It had no inflation factor built in and had started out as a reasonable royalty twenty-nine years earlier but by this time had declined to about .5 percent of sales. A typical industry royalty is three to six percent of sales. The chain was surviving essentially by the entrepreneurial gumption of our franchisees. Legally, we were a public company; functionally, we were a private company owned by the twelve men who sat on my Board of Directors. They were multi-unit franchisees who owned seventy-two percent of Sonic. Less than ten percent of our stores had cash registers, so we were not getting meaningful purchasing and marketing data. And our operators did not know we were going out of business.

Being thirty-six and too ignorant to know it couldn't be fixed, I went to Sonic with a lot of enthusiasm. Strategically, the three most important issues were: First, to get the chain united in advertising and purchasing and operating like a chain. If we could not accomplish this nothing else mattered. Second, to put a new royalty licensing agreement in place—otherwise, as we fixed the chain, the franchisor would not reap its share of the rewards. Third, the most urgent thing was to stop the annual hemorrhage of a million and a half dollars in company-owned stores.

We focused on the markets where we had a critical mass of stores, such as Joplin/Pittsburgh, Missouri and Jackson, Mississippi. The franchisees in each market would come together for a day. I would graphically prove to them that we were going out of business. Once I could see reality dawn in their eyes, I would say, "The good news is, we are going out of business slowly, and, if you will take a step of faith with me, we can fix this together." The objective was to establish twenty-one advertising/purchasing co-ops in about one-third of our system and show the rest of our operators the power of uniting in order to create a critical mass that would drive same-store sales growth and reduce food cost. Further they were required to sign up at least seventy-five percent of the stores in that co-op's marketplace.

We knew critical mass in each co-op was a necessity. I asked the franchisees to sign a simple six-page legal document committing to each other to form a purchasing and advertising co-op for one year. They would purchase from one distributor of the co-op's choice and commit to spend one percent of sales on advertising. After a year of hard work, we did not have twenty-one co-ops formed, but we had seventeen and put our complete focus on making those perform.

Increasing the royalty was a political challenge because the majority of our stock was owned by franchisees. The way we sold this was to convert to an industry standard percent of sales royalty but make it a graduated scale. So we started at .5 percent (about what they were paying) and went up to four percent as sales went up.

The third piece, the most urgent piece, was fixing the bleeding in company-owned stores. We required the managers of the 110 company-owned locations to buy twenty-five percent of their unit, essentially converting them to partners and the CEO of their store. Turnover rate went from 110 percent a year to eight percent.

Owner-managers became the star of the show at annual conventions. The first "Manager of the Year" was a little five-foot six-inch guy in Southern Kentucky. His store showed two years of positive sales. On a $28,000 annual salary, he made $240,000. What did that say to every other manager in the audience? "If he can do it, I can do it!" It was a magical thing. I asked how he did it. "I reached a point of understanding that this was my business and not yours," he replied. "I reached a point of more fear about failure than fear of people. I got out of my store and everywhere I went I was the Sonic brand."

Local store marketing exploded in a positive way.

By the time I left twelve years later, ninety-eight percent of the chains purchased together and ninety-four percent of the chains advertised together. Average store sales moved from $210,000 to breaking all industry records for consecutive years of same-store sales growth, and currently average about $1.1 million per store. The year before I left, *Success* magazine chose this old, weary, worn out, fifties-style restaurant chain as the number one franchise opportunity in the world. And in recent years, Sonic has reached a market value of about $2.3 billion. It was a wonderful run. Again, I say turnarounds are a "we" thing, not a "me" thing.

Because of the way God blessed us at Sonic, I was invited to take on another turnaround challenge: Shoney's and Capt. D's, headquartered in Nashville, Tennessee. Over my three years at Shoney's, we put together a new management team and strategic plan. We were chipping away at it. Shoney's same-store sales had dropped significantly in the four years before my arrival. By my final eighteen months, we moved that to negative one percent with occasional positive months. We moved health inspection scores from a miserable sixty-seven to a healthy eighty-nine, and our stock price from about $7 to $13.

Could we have fixed it? I don't know. However, the co-founders owned eighteen percent of the company and were impatient about the turnaround. They began an effort to regain control of the company through a proxy battle. A few months into the battle, we reached a negotiated settlement. After this, I decided to depart the company. In the world's eyes Sonic was enormously successful and Shoney's was not. But in my heart, I had some of the most fun and did some of the best work of my career at Shoney's.

4

SUCCESS
"MORE THAN PROFIT"
▼

Jeff loves to be around people and so he chose to work in the restaurant business instead of a desk job. He feels called to be a missionary in his own backyard. Jeff uses his gift and passion for business and people to glorify God in the three Chick-Fil-A restaurants he owns.

Scan QR Code to see the Video
or go to:

http://www.rightnow.org/wawbook

CHAPTER FIVE
MONEY $

"No one can serve two masters. Either he will hate the one and love the other, or he will be devoted to the one and despise the other. You cannot serve both God and Money."

Matthew 6:24

These words of Christ are as challenging as they are confusing. I'm always suspicious when I hear someone say they don't care about money. "How do you live without it?" I want to ask. Nevertheless, Christ's words hang in the air, needing to be dealt with. If there is one criticism of business, it's that it's all about the money. Jesus is saying we need to be all about God.

Money is something we all need, and most of us have to work for it. If entrepreneurs and executives did not go to work everyday creating wealth, human suffering would be the inevitable result. Our basic life necessities, such as food, shelter, and water, all require money. As we move beyond these basic necessities to other valuable activities, like education, transportation, hobbies, family trips, more money is needed. How do we reconcile this reality with what Jesus says?

Deep down most of us want more money than we need. Therein lies the tension—we need money, yet we want even more. When it comes to money, motivation and focus are significant issues. If we work solely for money, then we have not understood the divine and spiritual purposes for work. If all we seek is money, then we are never satisfied. They say John Rockefeller, the world's first billionaire, was asked how much money it takes to make one happy. "A little bit more," he supposedly replied.

Money is like air. It is necessary for survival but should not define our purpose. If we are living to breathe, are we really even living? If we are living for money, are we spiritually alive?

Due to its centrality to our lives, money is a topic on which we should begin to formulate some serious thoughts. Conclusions regarding money are hard to come by, but the goal of this chapter is to get the conversation moving in the right direction.

KEN ELDRED on
THE MYTH THAT POVERTY IS NOBLE

It is a commonly held myth that Christians ought to embrace poverty as if poverty is somehow noble. If a person makes any money, it becomes a guilt trip. You don't really want to talk about your business success. The impact of this myth is probably best illustrated in a note a young man wrote me:

> *I wish I had read your book four years ago. I became a Christian during my first year at the MIT business school program. I believed I had to leave business and go to the mission field. Making money was just not appropriate. I just came back a year ago after three years in the Philippines, and I returned a broken man. This wasn't what I was supposed to do. Now I am working as a consultant for a major company just trying to get my feet back on the ground.*

When we buy into conventional wisdom, whether it is supported by the church or not, and we don't check it against Scripture, we end up going to places where we should not.

When the Soviet Union developed in the 1900s, the Christian community bought into the nobility of poverty, that everyone should have the same thing. People look at the world with rose-colored glasses—a tint that isn't natural. We embraced the idea that business is a zero-sum game. What is that? Poker is the perfect example of a zero-sum game. Everybody starts with the same number of chips. However, when the game is over somebody's got more and others have less. That is not what God created in business. Deuteronomy 8:18 says, "Remember the LORD your God, for it is he who gives you the ability to produce wealth."

In the parable of the rich man who had made a lot of money in agriculture, the man said to himself, I know what I will do, I will tear down my barns and build bigger ones and have food and wine to drink for the rest of my days. To which, the Lord said, "You fool! This very night your life will be demanded from you. Then who will get what you have prepared for yourself?" (See Luke 12:16-20.)

Building and creating wealth increases the size of the pie. Another way we used to say it is that the rising tide lifts all boats. Creating wealth lifts all boats. It is an important concept as opposed to buying into poverty. Poverty is a curse, not a blessing according to Deuteronomy 28:15 (NLT): "But if you refuse to listen to the Lord your God and do not obey all the commands and decrees I am giving you today, all these curses will come and overwhelm you."

There are so many verses about wealth. Being wealthy isn't the issue. It is how you acquire it and what you do with it that counts--how you respond to who God is in your life. Ask yourself, "What role does wealth play relative to my faith?" As long as it doesn't get in the way of your faith, and as long as you are ready to do whatever God calls you to do with what he has given you, wealth is not the issue.

HOWARD DAHL on
GREED

Greed has no limit. Just because someone has a lot of money doesn't mean they can't be extremely greedy. I know people who feel poor because they only have a small plane and not a Gulfstream. Greed and envy don't know socio-economic boundaries.

A big part of the current economic mess is that leaders were very greedy and couldn't have cared less how their decisions affected others. I think much of the problem is the consolidated debt obligations. Most people didn't understand them. Leading agencies were either ignorant—not understanding them—or they were evil—closing their eyes and giving high ratings to instruments that were shams. I'd like to think they were ignorant and not malicious, but who knows what was in their heart.

SCOTT HARRISON on
THE STORY OF charity : water

When I was four years old, my conservative Christian parents and I moved from our home in Philadelphia to an "energy efficient" home in New Jersey. Unfortunately, not even the inspectors noticed the four quarter-sized cracks in our gas furnace. While my dad was working and commuting, and I was outside playing with friends, my mom was in our home breathing carbon monoxide day in and day out. Finally, she collapsed and was rushed to the hospital with carbon monoxide poisoning. It was too late to reverse the damage. Mom went from a healthy young woman to an invalid whose immune system saw all chemicals as the enemy. For the rest of her days, she was allergic to anything chemically based.

Moving forward to my teenage years, I was the ideal Christian son, active in youth groups and Bible study, pretty good in school, no problem to my parents, helping with Mom's care. Home life was unusual. My mom basically lived in our tile bathroom with foil on the door to keep out the fumes of the stain that had been used on the door five years earlier. To talk with her face to face, we had to go out into the yard and I had to stand downwind so no chemicals from my clothes, etc. would reach her. My clothes had to be washed in baking soda. Life revolved around providing a toxin-free environment for my mother.

At eighteen, I joined a rock band and moved to New York City to become rich and famous and rebelled against the disciplines of my faith. I wanted to do everything I had been told I couldn't do. I dove deeply into the New York nightlife. Our band was talented musically, but challenged relationally, and we eventually split up. I noticed that the guy who regularly booked our band worked very little and made lots of money. I liked that combination and figured I could pull it off. I began working at a club called Mel's on 14th Street. We were successful in promoting a high level R&B open mic night, pulling in folks like Stevie Wonder and Prince. Many incredible singers came through the club.

During the few years I worked at Mel's, I went to college part time. I didn't live on campus and gave college just enough effort to make my dad happy, barely pulling Cs in my classes. Our promoting services morphed from Mel's R&B scene to the fashion world at a club just around the corner from my apartment. Models, celebrities, and stars were drawn to this club. Soon, I was being paid $2,000 a month to drink Bacardi products at the club and Budweiser also paid me nearly $2,000 a month to down Bud during parties. Ironically, we were considered "influencers" when we were actually just people who partied hard. The clubs were high end, selling $300 bottles of vodka and $15 drinks.

Almost a decade into this life, I began to feel numbness and tingling in my arm and submitted myself to a battery of tests for MS, Parkinson's, diabetes, and anything else the doctors could think of. Though they found nothing wrong and the tingling went away, I was suddenly touched by my own mortality. A few months later, a group of my partying friends, my girl-friend at the time, and I rented a gorgeous house in Uruguay for a month. It was the perfect place for God to get my attention. I would party 'til five in the morning, and then read A.W. Tozer and the Bible all afternoon. A push-pull for my soul had begun.

I realized I had become the most selfish, arrogant, miserable person I knew. Many of the people around me weren't exhibiting the values of my faith, which I'd covered up but still held deep down inside of me. I hadn't yet be-come an atheist and completely walked away from my faith. I had simply walked away from obedience—very, very, very far away into a small cor-ner—but my faith was still there. During that vacation, I resolved to come back and live life differently, which was a challenge since I didn't know how to do anything other than what I had been doing the last ten years!

Back in New York City I floundered. I stopped doing drugs and tried to drink less, but wasn't very successful. Four months later, something happened in one of the clubs that made me see nightclub life for what is was. So I took a month off and went north to New Hampshire and Maine with my Bible in an effort to figure out what the Bible was saying to me personally. It dawned on me I did not have to go back to New York. I could do something radically different. After praying and searching and thinking, I decided, "Wouldn't it be cool if I made my life look just the opposite—serve God and the poor instead of only myself?" I got the dream to go to the poorest country in the world and serve the people there. The challenge was finding a Christian organization that would take me. Having a nightclub promoter on your roster was not what most mission groups were looking for.

So, I didn't go back to New York. Instead, I continued my search while staying with a friend in France. One group really struck me as "out there." They were called Mercy Ships. These served as floating hospitals for doctors and surgeons who used their vacations to fly to the poorest countries in the world and volunteer their time aboard a 500-foot long yacht remodeled into a medical center where they would operate on and give medical attention to the world's poor. Staff volunteers paid $500 a month to serve aboard the Mercy Ships. This definitely fit into the "opposite" box of the way I had formerly lived. ·

I applied for the only open position: photographer. I had no photography training but put together a nice portfolio of pieces from vacations, life, portraits, etc. With my "credentials," I didn't receive a positive response to my application, but as the photographer position remained open and the sailing date came closer, Mercy Ships contacted me in the south of France and asked me to meet them in Germany. They were very clear, "We aren't agreeing to take you. We are only agreeing to *meet* you." I needed to convince them that I wasn't crazy, I wasn't going to throw raves or otherwise corrupt the crew, and that I really wanted to serve God and the poor. A few weeks later, I was on the ship in our first port: Benin, West Africa. Our ultimate destination was Liberia, a country destroyed by war.

For eight months, my job was to photograph everything that happened on board the ships and out in the villages. On our third day, I looked onto the docks and saw 5,000 people lined up in hopes of becoming one of the 1,500 patients our doctors could care for. One fourteen-year-old boy, Alfred, overwhelmed my senses. There on the other side of my lens was a teenager with a face totally disfigured by a fourteen-pound tumor that was slowly suffocating him. His eyes radiated anger. I fell apart and had to find a corner to collect myself. The ship's medical director told me I'd see much more of that, but that Alfred's story would end well. And it did. Three weeks later I got to take Alfred back to his village. Today he is a strong, normal, happy young man.

I also got to witness thirty-year-old women blinded by cataracts precipitated by their traditional equatorial sun dancing, clapping, and able to see just one day after cataract surgery. Day after day the stories mounted.

It was during this time I began to understand issues around water. The Mercy Ships approach was, "We've got 300 volunteers. Let's make the greatest difference we can." So we went out to the villages to see what we could do. One of my best friends was a water engineer. Leif dug five or six wells a year. I was struck by the incredible impact a few thousand dollars could make when used to dig a simple well. A village of several hundred people could drink pure water instead of drinking from a disease-infested swamp. I learned eighty percent of disease on our planet is in some way related to unsafe water, lack of sanitation, or polluted water.

After nearly a year, I flew home and within an hour of landing in New

York, I was back up on a rooftop patio with a $16 margarita in my hand. My two worlds collided. Here I was holding in my hand a drink that cost as much as a bag of rice which would feed a family of four for a month in Liberia. It was too much.

The next couple months I ran around with my laptop telling the stories of the people whose lives were changed on the Mercy Ships. The Mercy Ships were virtually unknown, and I wanted people to hear about their work. The idea for an exhibition dawned on me. I was given space in a gallery and did an eight-day exhibition of the photos I'd taken during the previous voyage. People came, and we raised $95,000, which all went to the Mercy Ships organization.

But what was I going to do with my life after that? I decided to "follow the money." I went back to Mercy Ships to photograph what the $95,000 accomplished. I sailed with Mercy Ships for another year, following the medical work, and digging more water wells. After I wrapped up my two-year tour with Mercy Ships, I returned to New York and again faced the decision: What would I do with my life? I knew I would be doing work with the poorest of the poor for the rest of my

life, but my vision was a bit larger than Mercy Ships. I wanted to do something radically innovative, something that would have incredible impact.

At the same time, a lot of my friends were disenchanted with "charity" because most believed that only ten percent of what people give ever gets to those who need it. I saw an incredible opportunity to bring a large group of people back to the table, but we needed to reinvent charity and we needed to choose the issue of focus.

Water seemed the one issue that touched everything. Health is not the only thing affected by water. Women walking three hours each way to get a jerry can of muddy water have no time to build a micro-business or in any other way contribute to family funds. Girls lose their chance at education because they must spend their time collecting water for their families. Children miss months and years of school due to water-related illnesses. Health, economics, and education are all impacted by the shortage of safe water resources around the world. More than a billion people do not have access to safe drinking water. We wanted to reinvent charity, and we were all about water. What better name to give our group than "charity: water."

Nightclub promoters make a lot of money on their birthdays. They throw a big fling; then people come and buy their drinks. It's a lucrative night. We launched charity: water on my birthday, September 7, 2006, in a new club that had not yet opened. Seven hundred people came, paid $20, got a tour of the new club, and helped start charity: water. The $15,000 raised that night went to build six wells in northern Uganda. Every penny went straight to well digging. Charity: water was on the way!

Our one-hundred-percent model began that night. Every dollar donated for charity: water projects goes to clean water projects. Our administrative costs are paid from a totally different sector which donates specifically for that purpose. We felt if we were going to reinvent charity, it had to begin with what we did with the funds.

I went off to Uganda to work with local partners, photograph the sites before and after and provide living, real-time proof that our donors' dollars were making a difference. This has become another part of our business model. All our projects are equipped with GPS, cameras, and computers that are linked to Google Earth so that at any given time our donors can see what's happening at any project site.

Telling the stories has been our most important marketing tool. We want our website to be as compelling, edgy, and real—recognized as the best sites out there so that these stories can be seen and heard. The idea of giving your birthday for a well site and having folks bring $20 for charity: water has taken off and hundreds of thousands of dollars have been raised by people giving up birthdays, wedding gifts, even funeral donations. The first "Twestival" (or "Twitter-festival") was the brainchild of a friend of charity: water and was run totally independently by volunteers in various locations around the globe. We have done public service announcements (PSAs) and had films at the Sundance film festival. People can understand and see the impact of clean water sources through the stories we tell and that has grown our cause over and over again.

Choosing the countries in which we work is a matter of identifying the countries where water is scarce, ruling out countries at war because we don't have proficiencies for war zones, ruling out countries that don't want help, and then beginning to set up a working structure with countries, finding local help, and creating partnerships.

In the field, the work is done totally by local partners. We may interview three or four national companies that have been drilling wells, protecting springs, and/or creating bio-sand filters for ten to twelve years. We select the most exceptional company and begin to work with them, first on small projects and then expanding their projects and influence as our relationship grows. Some have now been responsible for over $5 million in projects.

When we have funds for one hundred wells and a need for five hundred, our local partners are the ones who look into the situation in each village—ground water, rainwater, current quality of the water, everything. They are the ones who triage the sites with the most needy and likely sites coming first.

Our five-year plan is to raise $200 million to reach ten million people. That's just a tiny percentage of the 1.1 billion without safe water, but it's a start. We believe we can provide safe drinking water to every person on the planet in our lifetime. It's certainly a goal worth giving my life to and I can't imagine ever doing anything else.

MONEY

"BUILDING GOD'S KINGDOM"

In this real-life story, learn how one major construction firm, Betenbough Home Builders, intentionally invests their lives and their profits into their people and into Kingdom work.

Scan QR Code to see the Video
or go to:

http://www.rightnow.org/wawbook

CHAPTER SIX
STEWARDSHIP

"For what does it profit a man to gain the whole world, and forfeit his soul?"

Mark 8:36 NASB

In the business world there is an emerging social consciousness, referred to as Corporate Social Responsibility (CSR) or the triple bottom line, denoting measurable financial, social, and environmental outcomes for business. In addition to making a profit, there is increased awareness that we need to take care of one another and the environment in order for humanity to flourish.

Most people of faith are aware of their need to live and behave according to scriptural teachings. However, what is missing sometimes is the shift from thinking purely in terms of personal behavior to the collective behavior of an institution, such as a business, or of society.

In Scripture there is a pervasive principle—generally referred to as stewardship—that we are called by God to take care of what he has given us in terms of our skills, talents, finances, as well as our influence and impact on others. The workplace is a natural setting where we are able to steward those God-given resources individually and collectively.

We need to ask ourselves, "What does it mean to be a good steward in business?" With some imagination we can quickly see that business can be an instrument that empowers rather than exploits the poor, protects rather than degrades God's creation, and enables us to be all that God desires. The goal of this chapter is expand our vision and broaden our horizons for the good that business can do—and hopefully the beginning of a conviction that we are the people who can do it.

BLAKE MYCOSKIE on
FOR-PROFIT PHILANTHROPY
THE SUCCESS OF TOMS SHOES

I'm a serial entrepreneur, having started five companies in twelve years. In 2006, I was burnt out and traveled to Argentina to relax, explore, and soak in the culture. In the process, I met a few social workers focusing on some of the villages on the outskirts of Buenos Aires and asked if I could tag along.

In one village, I noticed most of the children didn't have shoes, and if they did, they were too small, too big, duct taped, or ancient flip-flops. It shocked me. In my experience, shoes didn't seem that expensive. My shock deepened when I examined their feet and saw cuts, infections, and infestations.

It struck me this problem should be easy to solve. The idea came to start TOMS Shoes, a company that matches every pair of shoes purchased with a pair of new shoes given to a child in need—one for one. As of August 1, 2009, TOMS has given away 150,000 pairs of shoes.

Overcoming challenges

When I got the idea for TOMS Shoes, I had absolutely no experience in the fashion or shoe industry. The businesses I had started were in the technology and media world. Nothing had prepared me for this. I'm very curious, an explorer, and when I find needs that aren't being met, I like to create businesses that meet them.

The learning curve was intense. In a short time, while I was still in Argentina, I met with shoemakers, canvas vendors, and hired interns in America. It was the hardest and the most exciting part of TOMS, starting a business in an industry I knew nothing about. It's been a wild ride, but one well worth it.

Focus on a sustainable business model

It was important to create a company that was sustainable, that would provide for others consistently. A nonprofit would have worked, but soliciting donors year after year was tenuous, if they lost interest in my charity—what then? The children would be without shoes. With a sustainable for-profit business model, TOMS is able to stick to its promise, consistently providing shoes to children in need. As long as we can produce a good product that sells, every sale means another child receives a pair of shoes.

Our customers get to be part of making a difference. They love the idea. We officially launched TOMS Shoes online and in a few Los Angeles stores on May 5, 2006. Booth Moore wrote an article about us that ran in the *Los Angeles Times* May 20, 2006, and we sold more than 2,000 pairs of shoes over the weekend! I hired three interns to take orders, and since I only had 200 pairs of shoes in my apartment, I returned to Argentina to produce more. It took three months to fill the backorders.

Giving equals success

It gives me satisfaction to know that children around the world are receiving a pair of TOMS shoes because of a simple idea I had in 2006. My parents always engaged us in community service through our church. I learned what it was like to help others and see the immediate effects of helping. When I went into business, I always wanted to incorporate giving into whatever I did, and to me, it is success to have managed to do that with TOMS. In a sense, it's allowed me to go into ministry without having to leave my passion for entrepreneurialism.

I experience a sense of success as well, when I see my employees and customers around the world join in the "One for One" movement. It's amazing to watch it grow.

TOMS has strengthened my faith. Being around the impoverished and seeing their love and joy, how happy they are with what they have, has given me inner happiness. Providing shoes and seeing how life-changing that simple act is makes me thankful for all of the gifts I have been given.

BLAKE LINGLE on
A FAITH-REFLECTIVE BUSINESS MODEL

My first business was Card Shop. I opened it in my parents' woodshed. We thrived for about two days. Shortly after we ran our first advertising campaign, a cardboard box on which we'd strategically painted "cards" and an arrow, the Boise Police shut us down for not having a business license—a crushing blow for a seven-year-old. The business did not recover. A boys-only superhero club took over the space.

My only goal for Card Shop was to sell enough cards to buy other cards. I had more goals when I started Boise Fry Company (BFC) twenty years later: making amazing fries and burgers and creating an ethical business, influenced by and representative of my relationship with Christ. The latter goal, to me, meant helping the poor, protecting the Earth, and treating people like Christ would.

Some of the poorest, most disenfranchised people in America right now are recently arrived refugees. Though the U. S. Government invites refugees to America, they are not entitled to the same government aid as Americans. Their aid ends six to eight months after arriving. Not only do they come from dire circumstances—from places like Somalia, Iraq, and Bhutan—but they're also forced into dire circumstances if they don't find a job quickly in the U. S. Unfortunately, given the current economy, finding a job is very difficult.

Providing jobs to refugees is one way BFC can help the poor. God commands us throughout the Old and New Testament to help the poor. God doesn't elaborate much on how to help; he just wants us to help. God also puts increased expectations on the rich and those in authority. I'm not a rich person—by relative American terms, anyway. I flip burgers for a living. However, as a business owner, I have the authority to provide jobs, and thereby income, to the poor. It's one way I can live out my faith.

Minimizing BFC's effect on the environment is another reflection of my faith.

There are many reasons why I feel we should protect the Earth.

1. The Holy Spirit is here amongst us, and just like us, he doesn't like seeing his surroundings polluted. He says so in Numbers 35:34 NLT: *"You must not defile the land where you live, for I live there myself."*

2. Evangelism. Earth's beauty, and the fact that we can appreciate it, is often cited as a means for understanding and acknowledging God. Romans 1: 20 (NLT) says: "From the time the world was created, people have seen the earth and sky and all that God made. They can clearly see his invisible qualities—his eternal power and divine nature. So they have no excuse whatsoever for not knowing God." I want the Earth to stay as pristine as possible, so people can see God.

3. The Earth is not ours to keep. God is permitting us to use it. "The Earth is the Lord's, and everything

in it," as it says in Psalm 24:1 (NLT). I know if God let me borrow his Pinto—I imagine God driving something humble—I would not return it with a flat. Nor do I want to return the Earth with a flat.

The hospitality industry is a big polluter, restaurants especially. Restaurants buy, make, and trash lots of products. When we started BFC, we made a decision to buy organic, sustainable, and biodegradable products, in an effort to become one of the only one hundred percent green restaurants in the United States. Some of our green products include biodegradable fry cones, napkins, and to-go cups. We also recycle some of our waste. Our excess potatoes are recycled to grow more potatoes and our used peanut oil is recycled in cars. And finally, we use Energy Star freezers and refrigerators and low-wattage, energy-efficient light bulbs. We're not fully green yet, but we're making progress.

Furthermore, a healthy Earth makes for a healthy body. Modern farming (some, not all) has extracted nutrients from food and replaced them with pesticides. That, coupled with the preservatives added to most processed foods, makes for unhealthy meals. In my opinion, pesticides and preservatives are as much to blame for obesity as saturated fats. Organic food is devoid of the pesticides that are polluting our bodies.

At BFC, when feasible and/or affordable, we purchase local, natural, and organic foods. We also prepare everything in house, which prevents the need for preservatives. Finally, we don't adulterate our humble fare with unnecessary ingredients and fat. Potatoes and peanut oil are the only ingredients in our fries. Other fast food fries have most, if not all, of the following ingredients: potatoes, vegetable oil, partially hydrogenated soybean oil, natural beef flavor, wheat and milk derivatives, citric acid (preservative), dextrose, sodium acid pyrophosphate (maintain color), dimethylpolysiloxane (antifoaming agent), and salt. Yikes! I'm no physiological expert, but I can't imagine that some of those ingredients are good for you. As it says in 1 Corinthians 6:19, our body is a temple, and though we understand that fries and burgers aren't the healthiest foods, we strive to serve the healthiest, most amazing fries and burgers around.

We also strive for amazing service at BFC. Toward the end of the movie *Family Man*, Nicolas Cage's character says this during a job interview, "Business is business. Wall Street, Main Street, it's all a bunch of people getting up in the morning trying to figure out how . . . they're going to send their kids to college. It's just people . . . and I know people." This quote often surfaces in my mind throughout the course of a business day. I'd like to think I understand people and that my understanding of people developed from my relationship with Christ. Christ gives plenty of advice on how to deal with people.

The second great commandment is to love your neighbor as yourself, so in some sense, by some transitive property, Christ gave excellent business advice. Understanding and appreciating people, both employees and customers, is the cornerstone for most ethical, successful businesses. Our service model at BFC is based on the second great commandment.

We recognize Christ was not and is not in the business of making money. I remember that when my relationship with Christ influences my business decisions. I also like to remind myself that anything he gives us, he can take away. We shouldn't use Christ as some business pundit for the accumulation of wealth. However, as Christians within the context of our business, we can have incredible impact on those around us. From customers to vendors to employees, we interact with lots of people on any given day, some may not know or believe in Christ. Interaction is our greatest witness. People won't attribute God to building a Fortune 500 company. People will attribute God to how you treat them. If you're involved in business, don't just sell a product to buy more products, like I did with Card Shop. We sell products because that's how we build our economy—but while selling products, we can let people see our relationship with Christ, because that's how we build the Kingdom.

KEN ELDRED on
PRAYING FOR BUSINESS

There is a prevalent myth that it's not spiritual to ask for specifics in prayer, especially in business. A friend of mine is a great example of this. He managed a small contracting group and had a measure of faith. It was fairly limited, but not unusual compared to a lot of business people who say, "I do pray, but I never pray about specifics. I pray that God's will be done and I pray that God will give me wisdom and strength and guidance." Conventional wisdom says that we pray about our spouse, our kids, people in the hospital, other folks, or our nation, but not about business. We don't want to pray about *that*.

I don't know what I would have done if God had not given us those $7,000 days (see the story in chapter one on "Calling"). We ended up depending upon God.

6

STEWARDSHIP
"INVESTING PROFITS IN PEOPLE"

The Red Dot 100X ministry started out of a dream to expand the successful Red Dot metal building manufacturing business into a ministry that serves others. They leverage their profits to help others and also help employees meet the needs of children at risk.

Scan QR Code to see the Video
or go to:

http://www.rightnow.org/wawbook

CHAPTER SEVEN
BALANCE

"Work for six days and rest the seventh so your ox and donkey may rest and your servant and migrant workers may have time to get their needed rest."

Exodus 23:12 THE MESSAGE

A friend of mine once took a pay cut to take a job where he would be expected to work only sixty hours a week. In some industries, like investment banking, people spend as much as 100 hours a week at work. A forty-hour workweek is hard to come by for most professionals. Add in commute time and it can feel like all we do is work, work, work.

There is a very real tension of how much is too much when it comes to the time we spend working. How can we balance work with other worthy responsibilities, like a spouse and children for those who have them? Maybe there is no real balance. I once heard a speaker say, "God worked six days; that's not balance!" Point taken.

Balance is a challenging term as it implies equitable division of activity. According to that interpretation, there really can be no work-life balance *per se*; it is more like work-life *tension*. However, we are whole people so our lives have to be lived in an integrated fashion, even though there will be tension. Do I work more, or do I go home and play with the kids? Today's technology enables us to work everywhere all of the time. In my grandfather's generation, although they worked six-day workweeks, when the sun went down the workday ended. We are living in the age of connectivity when all things are possible at all times of the day. Therefore we must increasingly grapple with how we balance work with the rest of life's responsibilities.

God worked and calls us to work, but God does call mothers to be mothers, fathers to be fathers, spouses to be spouses, and all of us to study his Word, go to church, and a host of other things that require time. Jesus modeled a life of diverse activity. The biblical account shows him celebrating at a wedding, sleeping on a boat, enjoying a dinner party, and retreating for prayer. If there is anyone who could have justified working all the time, surely it was Christ.

Followers of Christ, therefore, need to reflect on all of life's priorities and ensure that we don't let life slip by and in the end, realize that we misspent God's gift of time. Our allocation of time is similar to all of the other resources we have. It needs to be spent in accordance to godly values and principles.

No one achieves the balance of life perfectly. We are all a work in progress. Most executives and entrepreneurs acknowledge balance as one of the most difficult things to achieve. Nevertheless, this chapter contains a lot of valuable insights that are worth mulling over in our quest for properly spending our time.

HENRY KAESTNER on
FOUR CORE VALUES

Bandwidth.com, like any company our size, has a unique working environment. Projects get done in a particular way, communication happens in ways subtly different from other companies, and individual and teamwork patterns are unique to Bandwidth.com. In aggregate, all of this makes up our distinct corporate culture.

Three components primarily influence our culture: our values, our leadership, and our people. Of the three, our values are most important as they shape the other two.

David Morken and I want to see the same core values drive the company that drive our lives. That means we focus on faith, family, work, and fitness—in that order. We believe, if we balance all four well, and in that order, we'll be successful.

Faith

We firmly believe our success has come from God, and we work for his glory. It's impossible to spend any meaningful time with us and not know that our Christian faith is what guides and drives us. David and I don't pass out tracts at work; in fact, people from several different faith backgrounds are part of our team. I believe everyone feels valued and not judged.

We're always ready to share why we have hope, but it's most important for us to model faith as being what we live for. It's our faith that compels us to submit our products, services, and relationships to the highest standard—a biblical standard. Even though we often fall short, we are always aiming toward that goal.

Family

I came to North Carolina from New York. While New York City doesn't have a monopoly on the seventy-hour workweek, there are few places on Earth where that value (or anti-value) is more prominently on display. I know too many families and lives that have been shattered by overwork. David and I have nine children between us, and we're all too aware we have two hours at most to be a Dad each weekday. For us, it's the hours between 6:30 to 8:30 p.m. We cherish that time with our families and want our employees to be able to as well. There are no heroics in staying in the office late at the expense of family. We all have plenty of time to get back online once we've put kids to bed. That happens most nights. The one night it won't happen is "date night"—that's when I get to take the boys' mom out to tell her how much I appreciate what she does.

Without a firm faith and family commitment, the next value just doesn't happen.

Work

David and I love our work. We like to lead; we like to create and innovate. We like to compete; we like to win. We like to challenge those who work with us, just as they challenge us. We like to question; we like to listen. We can always be better, and we love that, too. Work is the manifestation of much of who we are.

Fitness

Work hard; play hard. David and I go on a run or a bike ride just about every lunch hour when we're in town. Our employees follow our lead, and depending on the day of the week, droves of co-workers will head out for a game of ultimate Frisbee or soccer on the fields near our office, or basketball on the campus court. Some of our best partner retreats and senior management trips have revolved around fitness. We've had epic trips to ride mountain stages during the Tour de France, surfed with our channel team in Costa Rica, and gone heli-skiing several times. Fitness, particularly when done in groups, provides some of our best camaraderie, exchange of ideas, and rest from work.

DAVID MORKEN on THE DISCIPLINE OF WORK / LIFE BALANCE AS A CEO

As a CEO, I'm as busy as I want to be. It can consume all my waking and some sleeping moments, if I let it. The work can become an idol that you worship morning, noon, and night, and the pace can be absolutely invigorating and seemingly fulfilling. Over the years, it has been important to establish balance. You can only sacrifice family, your walk with Christ, and your physical health for so long before it catches up with you. Work in entrepreneurial capitalist gear, pushing the pedal to the metal for too long, will catch up with you—and you *will* explode.

I get up at 6:00 a.m. and start work no later than 8:00 a.m., often over breakfast with another leader at Bandwidth, and I'm done at 6:00 p.m. In the middle of the day, I take time for a ninety-minute workout. That's important, and I fit it in about four days a week. I try to limit travel to no more than one night a week away from the family. It has been an intentional business discipline to maintain the middle of the day workout and take only the most important trips, as well as avoiding being away from home more than one night a week. Balance has to be "on purpose."

Balance comes into play in leadership. We have a lot to accomplish, at high cost sometimes. Without the love of Christ, I could destroy the families of a lot of executives here. If I work late, they work late. If I didn't kick them out at 6:00 p.m., they'd stay and work. When you have alpha-type, hard-charging men and women working together, and they're having a blast at what they do, they could easily work too hard at the expense of their families. It's because I have a Savior that I won't let the team burn themselves out. We actually have signs reminding folks to be home in time for dinner. (See sign on pages 144-145)

When we hired our Vice President of Strategy, he shared an office with me—which he still does. He had come from a firm where he charged hard, so I had to kick him out every day at 6:00 p.m. At first, he thought he must be doing something wrong, or that we were going to dock his pay, but he's come to understand the importance of balance. Now at 6:00 p.m., you'll find him making sure his team of eighteen is on their way out the door for home.

There is never an easy time to bring balance; you always have to do it now. Understanding and respect for the importance of family and life outside work versus a sole focus on creating value in the company is the essence of our leadership. Don't get me wrong. I'm a red-blooded, American capitalist. I love to create value and serve lots of customers. I love to be relevant and deliver a fantastic customer experience at low cost, but not at the expense of our team or the integrity of the families involved in supporting Bandwidth. I think that's how we create a Christian foundation for everything we do.

The Discipline of Family Times
My wife and I have six children ranging in age from four to sixteen, three boys and three girls. Early on, Chrishelle and I chose to establish certain disciplines to support our values as a family. For example, dinner as a family is very important to all of us.

Even though our children are in football, soccer, and other activities, we wait for everyone to get home and eat together, usually at least four times a week, and reserve one weekend evening (leaving one for sleepovers, etc.) to share as a family. In the evenings, I am one hundred percent Dad until bedtime. This is non-negotiable.

Being assistant coach for my sons' Pop Warner football team helps me stay connected individually with my sons. Between time on the field and driving to and from practice and games, we have been able to have great conversations and deepen our bond through the shared activities. My daughters play soccer. Saturdays usually find me on the field cheering them on. We are a part of our children's lives, and we wouldn't have it any other way.

Vacations and holidays are family affairs, too. We love to camp, backpack, fish, and climb mountains. We spend a lot of time in tents and enjoying the outdoors. For the first fourteen years of our marriage, there wasn't a night when both of us were away from our children, not because it was a rule, but because we simply enjoy our family that much. We'd rather be together.

One great activity our whole family loves is reading together. Books by C.S. Lewis, J.R.R. Tolkien, and Christian missionary biographies are favorites with our kids. They often make an extra effort to be home for our reading time.

I can't say enough positive things about my bride of seventeen years. She is amazing. Although, Chrishelle and I don't have a "date night" practice, most evenings find us relaxing together and talking over the day after the kids are in bed. It's so intense with six children and the business—which can seem like a seventh, special needs child—every waking moment. We need to check the pulse on our relationship and each other's well-being. We're under so much logistical and time pressure, we can't afford to drift apart. Over this time we've learned to communicate with key words and phrases and accomplish quite a bit even in a brief exchange.

KEN ELDRED on
THE MYTH THAT CHRISTIANS MUST BE
THE LAST ONES OUT THE DOOR

A myth of conventional wisdom is that the serious Christian is somebody who will work significant hours—always going the extra mile, if you will. How can we truly be committed to our work and only work a forty-hour week?

When we were starting the computer supplies company, I was rather new in my faith. At a church retreat, I saw a verse on the logo of the Presbyterian Life Insurance Company: "If any provide not for his own, and specially for those of his own house, he hath denied the faith, and is worse than an infidel." (1 Timothy 5:8 KJV) It struck me as interesting. God is saying that we are supposed to take care of our family. I realized right there that he must have some set of priorities we should all be following. I wondered if there were others. As I searched, I stumbled on another verse dealing with priorities: "Seek ye first the kingdom of God, and his righteousness; and all these things shall be added unto you" (Matthew 6:33 KJV). The word "all" is not a limited word; the dictionary says it means "everything."

According to the Bible, setting proper priorities means putting God first—"Seek ye first the kingdom of God." That this should be our first priority is made clear. The verse from First Timothy above made me think that a close second is family, which means spouse and children. I interpreted "providing for" as encompassing all the needs of my family, including quality time, attention, relationship, and fun. After those foundational requirements are met, work—as in generating income—becomes a priority.

As a good MBA, I asked myself, "Okay, if these are the objectives, how much time do I need to spend with God every day? To build a better relationship with him? To love him more? To understand him more? How much time do I need to spend with my wife and children? What about my personal needs for rest and exercise?" I wrote down what was a reasonable amount of time for each of my priorities and added up the hours they would take during a five-day workweek. I put in eight hours for sleep a day. Then, subtracting the total from the number of hours in five days, I came up with basically forty hours a week left to do my work. It was clear that I could only be a forty-hour-a-week kind of guy in order to keep my priorities straight.

This choice had a couple of ramifications.

First, I realized venture capitalists expect you to put in anywhere from sixty to eighty hours a week. I talked to a couple who thought the idea of starting a business on forty hours a week was nutty. They didn't want any part of it. They didn't ask how many hours I would put in, but I answered before they asked. The response was always the same: eyes glazed over as I heard something like, "Thank you for coming in to see us. Good bye." Without venture money, what were we going to do? We ended up borrowing from our families. Our plea came with the advice, "We don't really want you to invest because this is too risky." But you know how mothers are. Mine put some money into our company. I thought she was crazy, but she said, "I believe in you." We ended up with roughly $50,000 to start our venture. My contribution was $5,000 and a grocery bag of electronic parts.

Second, I had to decide what was important. When you have lots of venture capital, sometimes hundreds of millions of dollars, priorities are not as vital. Without a lot of money, you have to be careful. "What can I do to reduce the risk? What can I afford to do—and what can I afford not to do?" Defining our limitations meant that we had to think very carefully about who we wanted to be as a business.

Each workday was very intense because I only had a few hours to do it in. I had to learn how to delegate. I doled out responsibilities, "You are going to do shipping, and you're going to do ordering and accounting. You are going to manage receiving." My staff finally looked at me and asked, "Well what are you going to do?" I told them that I was going to write the next catalog because that was our future. If the catalog drove the business, the other things just had to follow along. The result was that we had more "sweat" equity in the company, and we had more committed employees who really took ownership in the business.

7

BALANCE
"WITNESS AT WORK"

Sandy is an air traffic controller at a major metropolitan airport. He shares how perseverance in sharing the gospel and building friendships at work led to the unlikely conversion of a co-worker who was boldly anti-religion.

Scan QR Code to see the Video

or go to:

http://www.rightnow.org/wawbook

CHAPTER EIGHT
RELATIONSHIPS

"Let us consider how we may spur one another on toward love and good deeds. Let us not give up meeting together, as some are in the habit of doing, but let us encourage one another."

Hebrews 10:24-25

One of the great travesties of original sin is what it did to our relationships. As soon as God confronted Adam and Eve about who ate what, Adam started to point the finger at Eve. Shortly thereafter we read of Cain killing Abel and after that it only got worse. We humans have had a hard time with relationships ever since.

When I talk with people who are struggling in their faith, they frequently communicate that they feel as if no one understands them. When I talk to people who are strong in their faith, they frequently point to a group of close-knit relationships they have developed as the key to their success. Without relationships, we feel isolated and alone. With negative relationships, we are pulled away from what is noble and worthy. With positive relationships, we prosper and become the better for it.

We were created to be in relationship—to be in community with one another. Consistently throughout the Scriptures you see the story of God revealing himself among people living in community who, despite their proximity, frequently don't get along. Relationships will never come easily, but the wise person realizes our need for them.

Our lives are a web of relationships. We need all kinds of relationships: peer relationships, mentor relationships, mentee relationships. The strongest relationships tend to be with people with whom we've shared an experience or have something in common. It has been my experience that marketplace people need to be in relationship with one another in a unique way. They are enduring the same pressures, passing through the same experiences, and feel alone just as much as anyone else. This chapter should encourage us all to take a look at our relationships and be intentional about the ones we develop.

ED MEESE on
RONALD REAGAN AS A MENTOR

My most significant mentor was obviously Ronald Reagan. He was more than a person I worked for; he was a mentor from whom I learned a great deal over the thirty years that I worked with him.

Our first meeting came out of the blue. In December 1966, Reagan, having been elected Governor of California, was assembling his staff. I was very happily practicing law in a district attorney's office in Oakland, California. I seemed to be doing well and thought I would spend the rest of my life there. However, somebody remembered my representing all the district attorneys and chiefs of police in California before the state legislature on criminal justice and procedure matters six years earlier. That person recommended me to the incoming governor, and I was asked to meet Reagan and his staff in Sacramento. In the half-hour interview, I was deeply impressed with Governor Reagan—not only his personality, but also the depth of his knowledge about criminal law and criminal justice. We had different ideas about those topics, but our viewpoints meshed. At the end of our meeting, he offered me a job, and I accepted on the spot. I drove home trying to figure out how to explain to my wife that we would be moving to Sacramento. About thirty years later, in September 1997, I visited Reagan for the last time, just before he went into total seclusion due to Alzheimer's disease.

My tenure with Reagan was a tremendous opportunity to learn from a man who also held many positions during his life. He was an Army Reserve Officer and served in World War II. He had been a movie actor, a radio sportscaster, a newspaper columnist, and president of the Screen Actors Guild labor union. He was involved in a variety of political activities, both as a Democrat and as a Republican. He became California's governor, and ultimately, President of the United States. In all of those jobs, he was always concerned about other people, and he was always guided by his religious faith.

People often ask, "What was Ronald Reagan really like?" His tremendous cheerfulness and optimism distinguished him as a leader. I can't remember a time when his optimism didn't surpass the greatest difficulties and even the darkest days that he faced as governor of California or President of the United States. Reagan's cheerfulness was reflected in a tremendous sense of humor. He used jokes and stories to relieve tension, make a point against an opponent, or enliven a speech. It was just part of who he was. If a cabinet meeting got tense and people were at each other's throats, he would often tell a joke so people left the room in a more relaxed frame of mind.

Reagan's optimism did not disregard what was going on around him, the consequences of his decisions, or the tremendous problems that were facing our country. The 1980s were marked by the country's worst economic conditions since the Great Depression. Unemployment was rising beyond 7.5 percent to ten percent, inflation was 12.5 percent, and interest rates were at twenty-one percent. We had a stagnant economy—*stagflation* they called it—something economists previously thought couldn't happen. A tremendous energy shortage was also in full swing. You had to wake up at 5:00 a.m. to line up at a gas station because by 8:30 a.m. the gasoline would be sold out for the day. Those were the conditions that Reagan dealt with, but he was optimistic because of his tremendous faith in God. You don't read much about that because he felt religion was a very private matter. He was not unwilling to discuss it with anybody who raised the topic, but he tried not to raise it deliberately himself because he didn't want people to think he was trying to use his religion for political purposes.

Yet religion was so much a part of Reagan's life that if it came up in conversation, he was able to quote the Bible like very few people I have ever known. He often used religious subjects as illustrations in his speeches. In fact, Reagan made more references to religious or biblical subjects in his speeches than any other U.S. president. In March 1981, as Reagan was recovering from an assassination attempt, he wrote in his diary, "I believe that God has some important things for me to do, and that is why I was spared." From that point forward he had an additional sense of purpose for his life. One of his goals was bringing peace to the conflict with what was then the Soviet Union, a part of history he was primarily responsible for achieving.

ED MEESE on PRAYER BREAKFASTS and SMALL GROUPS

It's surprising how many prayer groups there are throughout Washington, DC, including in the U.S. Senate and the House of Representatives. Prayer is one of the few mediating forces at the height of tensions between people of differing political parties and political views. At the weekly Senate and House prayer breakfasts, you will find some of the most virulent partisans on one side of an issue sitting down next to people equally adamant on the other side of the issue. For that hour that they are together, they have a very different attitude towards each other, and to some extent, I believe that spills over into the rest of their day.

You can find many outstanding examples of people in various professions, but particularly in politics, who have been guided by—rather than impeded by—their religious principles. People who also have been willing to take action, sometimes even against the best interests of their so-called political fortunes, on the basis of their religious principles.

I have traveled around the world addressing prayer groups, and I have found that religion means especially a lot to people in the military. The military seems to have a high percentage of people who practice religion. I spent a great deal of time in the military myself, and my son is now a military officer.

In the fall of 1982, a very religious, long-time friend asked if I would be interested in joining a weekly small group for prayer, fellowship, and Bible reading. This was during a very difficult time in my life. My family had recently lost a son in an automobile accident. On top of that, there was significant in-fighting in the White House, and sometimes I became the target of newspaper articles. So I was willing to give the group a try.

My friend told me to be at the Pentagon the next morning at 6:30. I wasn't quite sure what I had signed up for, but I obliged and met my friend and two other men on the Pentagon's steps. We were taken to the office of the Chairman of the Joint Chiefs of Staff, General Jack Vesse. He was the highest-ranking military officer in the United States Armed Forces. When the four of us got together, we mostly talked about our faith and the problems we each faced in our positions. It was a terrific opportunity to get to know each other better.

Up until this point, the Chairman of the Joint Chiefs of Staff and I had sat across the table from one another for several months on the National Security Council, yet I had no idea he was a person of great religious faith. I found we were both Lutherans, and in fact belonged to the same branch of the Lutheran Church. It was a tremendous blessing getting to know him. We have become great friends over the years and worked together on boards of directors of several corporations after he left the Army and I left government.

By 1985, General Vesse had retired from the Army, and I had become Attorney General, so we moved the prayer breakfast to my office. We changed it to 7:00 am Tuesdays and added a few new members. Being in this kind of intimate prayer group offers an experience that I have rarely found any place else. People can say anything and they know it won't be used against them. We make ourselves vulnerable—telling things that we wouldn't tell anybody else in the workplace, maybe things that are even hard to bring up at home—because the other people can relate to what we are going through. In that group, we could talk freely and solve a lot of challenging problems.

For example, one of the most difficult moral issues that I faced was when a former President of the United States wanted to know about a certain political figure who had worked for me. He had been extremely disloyal, had done a bad job, and had some real character defects. The dilemma was: how do you give an honest account to someone who needs to know about this person and yet not have it reflect your personal animosity? How do you do that with a person you have forgiven? We talked that over in our group for about an hour, and they gave me some helpful ideas. I was able to give an honest answer about this person that was consistent with my belief about how a Christian should walk in the love of God.

We decided to expand our group to foreign ambassadors willing to meet together in the name of Jesus. As a result, our Tuesday meetings brought together anywhere from four to ten ambassadors. It has been amazing for me to see the Christian faith that some of them brought with them. And that others, Muslims, Jews, and people who don't ascribe to any particular religious faith were also willing to come together in the name of Jesus. It is probably one of the more ecumenical events that take place in Washington, DC. We are able to talk about international affairs, poverty in certain countries, and so on. We can talk about these things in the spirit of Christ, regardless of people's own particular religious backgrounds. However, we have found that the larger group did not lend itself to the intimacy we found with the smaller group, so six or seven of us also meet an hour before the larger gathering.

I was once at a fairly large prayer meeting with close to twenty attendees in Jamaica. They told me that half of the people were on one side of the political aisle and half were on the other side. They were mortal enemies in the legislature. The prayer meeting was the one place they could gather in peace and relative harmony.

The three ingredients that all of these small groups have in common are:

1.   Candor. Nobody is putting up a front or holding anything back. Everyone is honest.
2.   Confidence. Assurance that what is shared will stay
within the group, and people are there to help and support each other.
3.   Comradeship. The genuine fellowship that you have
with people whom you totally trust, whom you totally
like, and with whom you can exchange confidences.
These people can help you find solutions.

If I could give one piece of advice to all of you who will someday be the
magnates of the business world, it is to find a small group of confidants
with whom you can have this sort of relationship. It will be beneficial to
you throughout your career and throughout your life. The small group
does not necessarily need to be composed of all men or all women, or
only people who are in the same age-range or stage of life. Sometimes
it is easier for men, in particular, to talk with other men, and it would
be harder for them to share openly about their struggles if women were
around, but there is no reason the small groups have to be set up one
way or another.

One great experience was in a small group that traveled around Oregon encouraging the formation of these groups among business people. It included
three of the most important CEOs in the western part of the United States.
One was the owner of a very profitable string of restaurants, another was one
of the four co-chairman of the Nordstrom's retail chain, and the third was the
president of one of the most important banks in the Midwest. This opportunity to work together with these fine men and to spread the word about
small groups was a great opportunity for friendship and living our faith.

Reinforcing Relationships

The other thing that I want to mention is what I call *reinforcing* relationships. They can be small groups or people with whom you work. In the White House, although we didn't plan it this way, and we didn't have a religious litmus test in hiring, it seems the people who were attracted to these jobs had, for the most part, a strong religious background. You can't always decide who you are going to be working with, but certainly we can encourage colleagues who are of a similar religious faith. It is important in the difficult moments to have people who will support you in creating a workplace atmosphere that is not hostile to people of faith.

Unfortunately, there are workplaces—some of which are encouraged by state laws—that are almost hostile to religion. It is vitally important that people in positions of responsibility make sure this doesn't happen and encourage people in their personal religious faith and practices, as far as such encouragement is within the law and is done without showing favoritism.

Throughout my career people prayed for me, for my family, and for people who were working with me. It is amazing and hugely encouraging when people would recognize me on the street or write to me saying, "I want you to know that I am praying for you." Whenever the newspapers reported on a very tough issue that I was involved in as Attorney General, I would receive a plain envelope with no return address from San Diego, California. Inside would be a piece of lined paper on which was written nothing more than "Psalms 91." That is a powerful Psalm, in which David writes:

> *He who dwells in the shelter of the Most High*
> *will abide in the shadow of the Almighty.*
> *I will say to the LORD, "My refuge and my fortress,*
> *my God, in whom I trust." . . .*
> *Because you have made the LORD your dwelling place—*

the Most High, who is my refuge—
no evil shall be allowed to befall you.

Psalm 91:1-2, 9-10 NKJV

Well, it was kind of comforting just to get that plain piece of paper with Psalms 91, which would remind me again to read that Psalm. It was a tremendous source of support for me.

JEFF RUSSELL on CREATING A PLURALISTIC BUSINESS CULTURE

Easy Office is a social venture providing affordable finance, accounting, and bookkeeping services to nonprofits nationwide. We are a business service provider, i.e., an outsourcing company that sells people's time and expertise. We have no research and development department, no real fixed assets, no patents, no unique technology. As a people business, human resource (HR) strategy is front and center as the most important aspect of our success. Our business is based on identifying a neglected market niche, building a business model to support that market niche, and creating the operational platform and team to deliver to that niche. Creating the team to do that is my most important job as CEO.

I have grown up and lived by the Christian faith tradition all of my life. Being raised in the Deep South Bible Belt, growing up in this tradition comes as no surprise. Since leaving the South and traveling the world, I have continued to strive to live out my faith daily. After I graduated from college, I wrestled with whether I should be a missionary to the tribes of Papua New Guinea or if I should be a businessperson. I thought it was an either/or decision. Through a series of events, I came to realize that this choice did not have to be made; I could do and be both. I worked in the business world for ten years accumulating experience as a consultant, and then ran the Asian division of a multi-national company in Bangkok.

While in Bangkok, I looked out the windows of my twenty-seventh-floor, air-conditioned office onto a four-square-mile slum community home to nearly a million people. During the day, I worked tirelessly to make sure shoeboxes showed up on time, the cost of leather for our clients was as low as possible, and the packaging wouldn't fall apart during transit. But in the quiet still moments, I would stare out of my window looking down at the slum community, wondering what difference I had made. Some kid in Des Moines had some sweet, inexpensive, athletic shoes. So what? The fire burned within me to be more directly involved in something social.

After Bangkok, I spent two years pursuing my MBA at Yale. The Yale School of Management tag line is "Leaders for Business and Society," so it was a perfect fit for me. I came in with the idea for Easy Office and took copious notes in every class, relating each lesson to what Easy Office should be. During this time, more than twenty people—about ten percent of my class—donated time to improving our business plan. As we developed that plan and reflected on its potential over the course of those two years, it became clear to me that our HR strategy was essential. I wanted to be very intentional regarding the culture we built. As a start-up, we had the unique opportunity to build something from the inside out.

The volunteer Yale team came from predictably diverse religious backgrounds. Our ranks included Hindus, Buddhists, agnostics, atheists, Christians, and Jews. I knew I wanted Easy Office to reflect this diversity on an on-going basis. Although my Christian faith is important to me, I know it is individuals who must embrace faith for it to be meaningful, not the institution they work for. A person is a Buddhist or a Christian; an organization is neither. It is possibly made up of people of a single religion, but the organization reflects the people, not the other way around. My goal was to build a company that was truly pluralistic, not secular. I wanted religion and faith to be something that was openly discussed, not something that was hidden under the table.

As a social venture working exclusively with nonprofits, we recognized that our clients' values often conflict with each other, and may conflict with our own personal values. We chose to embrace this reality, not fight against it. In every interview I conduct for Easy Office, I tell the following story:

> One of the unique aspects of Easy Office is that our clients
> may have views that conflict with each other, or conflict
> with your own. For example, I was in Bozeman, Montana,
> a few years ago, meeting with the Predators Conservation
> Alliance. They wanted to save the wolves. The next day I
> met with the Cattleman Ranchers' Association, and they
> wanted to shoot every wolf in sight. I'd love to have both
> as clients. I'm from Mississippi, and my grandfather had
> cattle, but there are no wolves there, so it is not an
> emotional issue for me even though it is a highly charged
> issue for some people.

At this point the interviewee typically laughs and says something like, "Yes, I'm a very open person and know that not everyone agrees with me." One interviewee—that I hired, by the way—told me that she worked for the Cattleman Association, and her family gets authorization from the government to hunt wolves from helicopters. She told me that she was willing to work with Predators Conservation Alliance, but that she wouldn't be donating any money to them!

The interview continues:

> To take it a step further, maybe wolves are not an issue you
> get emotional about, but when you get into religion and
> politics, people can be more sensitive. I come from a
> Christian faith tradition; Amy, my partner, is Jewish. Folks
> in the company come from all different backgrounds. We

also serve clients of varying religions. One is a missionary in Asia, and we put Bible verses on her donation receipts. We serve multiple Jewish nonprofits along with a nonprofit in New York City focused on advancing Muslim causes. We've sent proposals to the Society to Abolish the Death Penalty, and we've sent proposals to Prevention Works, a needle-exchange program. We have clients who seek to evangelize Mexico, and some that seek to provide more alternatives for people with alternative sexual orientation. Easy Office is a place where "cause" and "beliefs" are all out in the open. Because of our clients, we could have it no other way.

At this point, some interviewees squirm. Those we don't hire. Some have told me that they won't work for atheists or groups that promote controversial causes. Those we don't hire. But most people smile and acknowledge that they enjoy working with groups of differing views; they understand that working for nonprofits is different than working with restaurants or other small businesses, and most people express surprise and appreciation regarding our openness.

Any HR strategy is more than just "selection." It is also about retention, rewards and recognition, recruitment, training, and performance management. Dr. Jim Baron, Yale professor and HR guru, constantly beat us over the head that HR strategies must be tailored to each unique business strategy; they must be in sync with the business culture of each company. If longevity with clients is important, don't hire contractors to interact with your clients. If clients are extremely price sensitive, as nonprofits are, don't build an HR strategy around paying the highest wages in town.

We have worked hard to make sure our entire HR system stays in sync with those we serve. For example, we don't provide employees with Christmas Eve and Christmas day off. Those are certainly considered

American holidays, but are also uniquely Christian. What do our Jewish employees really care about Christmas and the birth of Jesus? So to be consistent, we allow three flex days from September to December that can be used for Christmas, Hanukkah, or to go skiing.

We pay below market wages, but try to make up for it with flexibility and other benefits such as providing a week of paid time off for people to volunteer at a nonprofit of their choice. People who don't value volunteering aren't going to value this benefit, are going to feel under-rewarded, and are going to self-select *out of* working for Easy Office. People who do value this benefit, will enjoy this perk, feel appropriately rewarded, and will self-select *into* working for Easy Office. These are exactly the type of people we want to attract.

The HR strategy of any social venture needs to be carefully considered. If it is a "business as mission" company that serves an expressly religious purpose, the HR strategy may be different than our own. We exist to help all nonprofits—regardless of cause or creed—become more effective and efficient.

If and when we come across nonprofits that I personally feel are violating some of Jesus' teaching, and they want Easy Office's help, we still help. We do so because I am personally convinced that we should be salt in the world, not excluding ourselves or hiding from the world. Jesus' example shows interaction with all types of folks from all walks of life and belief systems. My goal is to mold Easy Office to mirror this same spirit of love and inclusiveness. In doing so, I personally believe we are helping live out the words of Jesus in helping others to clothe the naked, feed the hungry, house the homeless, and to help the prisoners, widows, and orphans.

JOHN TYSON on
FAITH-FRIENDLY WORKPLACE

We experienced an interesting situation shortly after we first communicated our Core Values to our employees. The Tyson helpline got a call, "I'm an atheist, and you don't leave any room for the Muslims, Buddhists, Jews, etc." The caller's list included everything but Christians. It was a fair observation. As we prepared to respond, it became very clear to us that the purpose of a faith-friendly environment, one of our Core Values, is to allow *all* faiths to participate in the workplace.

Within our company of 107,000 folks, we have a variety of faith traditions, including Muslim, Jewish, atheist, and agnostic populations, but most of our team members are Christian, due to the location of our plants (across the South and the Midwest). Striving to be faith-friendly provides respect and room for all of these populations. Now, we have operations in Mexico, China, Brazil, and India, as well as Europe. As we strive to be a faith-friendly company and honor God, we're trying to create an environment where it is acceptable to live your faith in the workplace. Our hope is that different faiths will enter true dialogue instead of polarizing discussions.

The reason our chaplaincy program has grown at Tyson Foods is that it's a program of attraction. It's not required. It's not mandated. When we first started out, we only had five or six chaplains. Now, we have about 150 chaplains and other faith leaders covering sixty to seventy percent of our locations. We've had to go through some adjustments in our company because the marketplace has been a little tough, but one of the things company managers have chosen not to cut has been our chaplaincy program. It has taken on its own life and is an important part of who we are and how we live. That's a testament to what we can do as business leaders by trying to create an environment of permission for all faiths to coexist in the workplace.

We've worked purposefully to avoid establishing an affinity for one group over another. We are a faith-friendly organization that gives permission for all faiths, not just Christian or Islamic groups. It is an integrated deal—holistic to our organization versus an affinity for one group that puts people in a box. There's a tendency to create programs that isolate groups instead of a faith-friendly culture that integrates. You have to fight through that.

Our chaplains and leaders of other faiths are part-time with us and full-time within their own religious groups. One of the questions I ask all the chaplains is, "Why do you want to be a chaplain at Tyson Foods? Why would you want to do this, since you already have a full-time job at the church?" Most tell me the chaplaincy work allows them to get back to the front lines and carry their ministry into the workplace. It gets them out of being in the church building all of the time—i.e., checking the books in the pews and all the other duties that go along with being a minister of a church—and back to what they always thought they were going to do, which was to help people try to move forward in their day-to-day lives. Maybe Bill and Mary are having difficulties because Bill drinks too much or Mary is not being faithful, or their son's having a challenge with addictive issues. Our chaplains are there to help them walk through whatever they are facing five days a week instead of just one. We didn't have a great game plan to begin with, but this is the way the chaplaincy has evolved.

People ask how we justify the cost of a workplace chaplaincy. Our plants, which usually consist of between five hundred and one thousand team members, are very aware of cost and margins. If we make two to four percent profit, it's a good year. The fact that the chaplaincy has gone from six chaplains to one hundred fifty through voluntary participation by plant managers is a tremendous indicator of its value. The program allows for early intervention in conflict. Our HR folks are involved with insurance, claims, and team member guidelines. The chaplains give team members a confidential ear and have the time to sit and listen. We have not had a single manager opt out of the plan to save money.

There's now enough measured evidence to demonstrate the plants are healthier because we have these ministers around to take on some tough issues. Our workforce is semi-skilled to unskilled. We have eighteen different languages spoken in our plants as well as a lot of political refugees, people from Sudan, Somalia, and Central America, just to name a few. We are a micro-picture of what America looks like.

A few years ago, over in Sudan a helicopter got shot down while carrying a leader of a Sudanese tribe. Before we knew it, that issue came to the floor in a beef plant, which had a significant Sudanese employee base. One tribe thought the other tribe had shot down their leader. We weren't prepared for it, but because we had chaplains on the plant floor, we were able to enter the debate and have some cultural and religious familiarity with how to handle the issue. Another interesting dynamic is Sudanese men will not take orders from women, and we have a lot of women leaders in our plants doing quality assurance and supervising. The chaplains often help bridge these issues by encouraging dialogue.

Faith in the workplace can work anywhere. Here are some basic principles that have helped us: First, avoid getting pigeonholed as an "affinity" program. Second, try to create an environment in which all faiths are permissible, whatever they may be. Third, it takes core people, not only at the senior level, but in middle to lower-level management. They're the ones to take ownership.

When we started this program, I had many discussions about whether I should mandate the chaplaincy program, but my personal experience led me to let the program sell itself without forcing the issue. We let the managers start talking to each other. When they started to share what they saw, we heard anecdotal examples of how the atmosphere had changed on the plant floor, stories of people working together. That's how we've gotten to where we are. If it comes from the top down, people feel like you're pushing religion on them, and they don't buy in. When we gave it our support and just laid it out there, it started to build momentum and has carried itself without our giving it any more emphasis.

STEVE REINEMUND on
DIVERSITY IN THE WORKPLACE

A few years ago, I gave a half-hour talk about the importance of diversity in business to an audience of five hundred students at Stanford University. During the question-and-answer session, the first student said, "I am convinced that you believe diversity is good for business. My question is: Would you do it if it weren't good for business?"

I answered that diversity is important in business. However, the student stood up again and said, "You didn't answer my question." So I went back and tried to answer his question again. The next student stood up and said, "In all due respect, you still didn't answer that question." Despite that rough start we went on and had a great discussion, but it continued to bother me long after the session concluded that I hadn't been able to find the words to really express what I thought on that subject.

Several of my colleagues serve as sounding boards for me on different issues. I discussed the incident with them, but none of them were able to fully explain why I felt so uncomfortable expressing my dedication to diversity whether it was good for business or not. Then one day, while I was on my treadmill—which is where I do my best thinking—it became clear. I had only addressed the business side—the head side—of the issue. I forgot that most issues of any importance have both a head side and a heart side. Hopefully, the students realized I believed in supporting diversity whether it was good or bad for business, although I was unable to state that clearly. I had felt I was supposed to focus only on the business side, or the head side, so I was unable to adequately address the student's question because I wasn't answering from my heart.

Yes, diversity is good for business. There is no question about that, and my belief in that fact is rooted in my personal life story. Although I grew up with no money, I didn't realize I was poor. My family had very little, and it was tough at times, but I began to recognize that I had a chance at a better life when certain people began leveling the playing field for me and giving me a fair chance to compete with those around me. At those times, I knew my economic status did not need to determine my future.

When I ran for student council, for instance, all the other candidates were wearing sports coats as they gave their speeches, but I wasn't. So a teacher gave me his coat and leveled the playing field. Such opportunities planted the seeds for my commitment to diversity and memories like that still make me emotionally committed to diversity today.

For better or worse, our life stories—what we really believe and what is fundamental to who we are—become evident when we are leaders. As leaders in business and society, we have an opportunity to incorporate our moral and ethical values into the work we do. We have to find our own way while also setting an example for our employees. Being a CEO has allowed me to combine my personal ambitions, thoughts, and values with what was ultimately best for the business. It is a responsibility I can never take lightly.

RELATIONSHIPS
"MEANING IN WORK"

Jon always thought that he would go into full-time ministry, but the doors never opened. He found a job in sports medicine at a deaf school and soon realized that he was using his gifts and talents to give glory to God as he built relationships with the students.

Scan QR Code to see the Video
or go to:

http://www.rightnow.org/wawbook

WORK AS WORSHIP
CONTRIBUTORS

CONTRIBUTORS
(listed alphabetically)

MO ANDERSON

Strong, principled, and compassionate, Mo Anderson's personal integrity and unending drive are touchstones that have made Keller Williams Realty one of the most successful franchises in real estate history. She established her first real estate office, a Century 21 franchise, in Edmond, Oklahoma, in 1975; soon after, it was the third top-producing office out of 7,500 Century 21 locations in North America. In 1986 Mo sold her company to Merrill Lynch Realty, where she served as a district vice president until December 1989.

In 1992, Anderson became the first Keller Williams Realty franchisee outside of the state of Texas when she persuaded Gary Keller to expand his profit-share concept for real estate offices. She launched the Oklahoma region and became co-owner of two Keller Williams market centers in that state.

In January 1995, Anderson became president and CEO of Keller Williams Realty. Since 2005, Anderson has served as the vice chairman for the company. Her focus is on cultivating the unique culture of Keller Williams Realty.

Anderson founded KW Cares (501(c)(3) nonprofit organization) in 2002 to assist company associates and their families in need and raised millions for Hurricane Katrina relief. She has been named twice as Oklahoma's Women in Business Advocate of the Year by the U.S. Small Business Administration. In December 2006, Anderson was named one of *America's Top Twenty-five Influential Thought Leaders by REALTOR®* magazine. In January 2007, the Women's Council of REALTORS® featured her as one of *Real Estate's Most Influential People* in an article published in *Connections*. And, in 2008, Anderson was inducted into the prestigious *Hall of Leaders* by the CRB Council.

DENNIS BAKKE

Dennis Bakke co-founded AES Corporation, a global electric company, in 1981 and was president and CEO from 1994 to 2002, during which time he built the international energy company into a multi-billion dollar enterprise with 40,000 employees in thirty-one countries. Currently, he is president and CEO of Imagine Schools, operating seventy elementary and secondary charter schools in ten states.

His innovative and often provocative bestselling book, *Joy at Work: A Revolutionary Approach to Fun on the Job*, tells the story of the transformation he watched in businesses, plants, and people as he put into practice the purpose of making AES the most fun place to work on the planet. One plant's experience, in the former Soviet Republic of Georgia, was documented in the film *Power Trip*.

HOWARD DAHL

Howard Dahl is the co-founder, President, and CEO of Amity Technology, a Fargo, North Dakota-based manufacturer of farm machinery. Its main product is sugar beet harvesting equipment, which dominates a majority of the U.S. market and is the primary leader in the Russian market. In 2007, Amity entered the air seeder market, which was the primary business of Concord, Incorporated, the company Howard led from 1977-1996. Amity is also the world's leading manufacturer of agricultural soil sampling equipment. Amity sells products in more than twenty-five different countries of the world. A sister company, Wil-Rich LLC, is a leading tillage manufacturer.

Howard is a Director of the Federal Reserve Board of Minneapolis and is a member of numerous other boards. Howard and his companies have been featured in national publications (like *Inc.* magazine) and are the recipients of a variety of awards such as North Dakota Exporter of the Year, 1994; North Dakota Innovator of the Year, 1997 (UND Center for Innovation); North Dakota Agricultural Person of the Year, 2004; Fargo-Moorhead Business of the Year, 2005; and First North Dakota company to be the SBA Region VII Exporter of the Year, 2006. Howard has a BS in Business Administration from the University of North Dakota and a MA in Philosophy of Religion from Trinity Evangelical Divinity School. Howard and his wife, Ann, have three children.

KEN ELDRED

Ken Eldred founded many successful companies, including Ariba Technologies, Incorporated, the leader in the Internet business-to-business industry which has reached a market valuation of $40 billion; Inmac, which grew to $400 million in yearly revenues as the first business to sell computer products, supplies, and accessories by direct mail; Mysoftware Corporation, now called ClickAction; and Norm Thompson Outfitters, Incorporated, a direct mail, consumer specialty retailer of high-quality merchandise. In 1988, the Institute of American Entrepreneurs named Eldred "Retail Entrepreneur of the Year for the San Francisco Bay Area."

Eldred's book *God Is At Work: Transforming People and Nations Through Business* is a leading work in the movement to integrate faith and work. Eldred and his wife, Roberta, founded Living Stones Foundation, a public support organization created to support Christian work and charity around the world. He also serves as chairman of Parakletos@Ventures, a top-rated venture capital firm in the Silicon Valley, California. Eldred, and his wife Roberta have three sons and currently reside in Silicon Valley.

DAVID GREEN

David Green is founder of Hobby Lobby, the largest privately owned arts and crafts retailer in the world. The headquarters are located in a 4.2 million square foot manufacturing, distribution and office complex in Oklahoma City. Affiliated companies include Hemispheres,

EthnoGraphic Media, Crafts, Etc! and Mardel, a popular Christian office and educational supply chain found in seven states. Hobby Lobby also has offices in Hong Kong and Shenzhen, China. David remains chairman of the affiliate companies, the CEO of Hobby Lobby and a buyer of merchandise.

David & his wife Barbara are the parents of two sons and one daughter. Mart Green, C.E.O. of Mardel Stores, Steve Green, President of Hobby Lobby and Darsee Lett, Vice President of Art/Creative. Son-in-law Stan Lett is Executive Vice President of Hobby Lobby and nephew Randy Green is President of Crafts, Etc.

Currently David serves on the Board of Reference for Oral Roberts University in Tulsa, Oklahoma. He is a past Ernst & Young national retail/consumer Entrepreneur of the Year Award recipient and lifetime member of the The Entrepreneur of the Year Hall of Fame, which is part of the Entrepreneur of the Year Academy. Green is also dedicated to a myriad of ministry projects.

DAVE GIBBONS

Dave Gibbons is a Xealot and Founding Partner of The Awaken Group (http://theawakengroup.com), a global leadership development/consulting firm with expertise in global culture, strategy, innovation, and creativity. He has a passion to see organizations and leaders have a double bottom line: to make a profit and make a difference. He also founded a nonprofit global leadership development and ideation group called XEALOT (http://xealot.net) connecting resources to marginalized leaders.

He is also the founding pastor of Newsong Church, an international multi-site church located in such places as Thailand, India, London, Los Angeles, Irvine, Dallas, Mexico City, and Beijing. Newsong is considered one of the most innovative churches in America by *Out-*

reach Magazine. Dave also serves on the Board of World Vision U.S. The author of *The Monkey and the Fish*, Gibbons is a vision-oriented leader known for his insightful thinking on the future of organizations.

SCOTT HARRISON

In 2004, Scott Harrison left the streets of New York City for the shores of West Africa. For ten years, Harrison had made his living in the Big Apple promoting top nightclubs and fashion events, and for the most part living selfishly and arrogantly. He returned to his faith and chose to turn his life around by working with Mercy Ships as a photographer. After serving on the Mercy Ships, primarily in Liberia, Scott returned to New York and, in September 2006, founded charity: water, a nonprofit organization bringing clean and safe drinking water to people in developing nations.

In their first three years, charity: water has funded 1,549 projects in 16 countries, serving over 820,000 people. Learn more at www.charitywater.org.

HENRY KAESTNER

Kaestner joined Morken as Co-founder in 2001 when he merged Bandwidth International into Bandwidth.com and served as CEO until early 2008. In his position as Executive Chairman, Henry Kaestner works with partner David Morken on the firm's strategy, financing, and marketing functions. Kaestner also oversees the partnership's not-for-profit activities.

Previously, Kaestner was the CEO of Bandwidth International, an international wholesale telecommunications broker based in London, England. He also founded Chapel Hill Broadband. Kaestner was a founder and former President and CEO of Chapel Hill Brokers, an energy broker which achieved more than $50 million in daily trade volume on more than 150 transactions, for clients including Morgan Stanley and Merrill Lynch.

Together with business and ministry partner, David Morken, Henry has founded DurhamCares.org, an organization that seeks to engage residents of Durham and encourage them to immerse themselves in service to their city; and MinistrySpotlight.org, which seeks to identify best of breed, independent Christ-centered word and deed ministries around the globe.

Kaestner lives in Durham with his wife Kimberley and their three sons.

BLAKE LINGLE

Blake Lingle is the CEO of the Boise Fry Company. After spending many moons slaving for Uncle Sam, Blake left civil service to flip burgers at Boise Fry Company. Some call his fry and burger making skills ninja-like, others call his skills overrated—depends on whom you ask. When Blake isn't making delicious fries and burgers, he's questioning why squirrels can't be pets, listening to Christmas music, playing Tetris, and/or chilling with his beautiful wife, Andrea. Blake's belief in God and miracles was confirmed when Andrea agreed to marry him. Blake and Andrea live in Boise, Idaho, with their golden retriever aptly named Chase.

BRIAN LEWIS

Brian J. Lewis is Managing Partner of Cereus Partners, an advisory firm to corporations and philanthropic organizations in the areas of strategy, marketing focus, and message. A graduate of Fuller Theological Seminary, Mr. Lewis also serves on the board of HOPE International, a global microfinance organization.

A frequent public speaker, he lives with his wife Barbara on Orcas Island, Washington.

STEVE LYNN

Steve Lynn is majority owner and Chairman of Cummings Incorporated and CEO of Back Yard Burgers, Inc. He served as CEO of Shoney's Incorporated from 1995-1998, and Sonic Corporation from 1983-1995. Lynn is known for transforming Sonic from a declining fast-food chain to the nation's largest chain of drive-in restaurants, with almost $2 billion in annual sales. His steadfast belief in putting value first has allowed him to develop positive work environments wherever he has held a leadership position.

Lynn has served on numerous boards including the Oklahoma City Chamber of Commerce, Oklahoma State Chamber of Commerce (past chairman), The Salvation Army, Fellowship of Christian Athletes, Young Presidents' Organization (past chairman), Oklahoma Baptist Medical Center, the University of Louisville, The National Cowboy Hall of Fame, and the International Franchise Association. He and his wife, Milah, have been married for over thirty years.

EDWIN MEESE III

Edwin Meese III, the seventy-fifth Attorney General of the United States of America, is a prominent leader, thinker, and elder statesman in the conservative movement. Mr. Meese holds the Ronald Reagan Chair in Public Policy at The Heritage Foundation and is the Chairman of Heritage's Center for Legal and Judicial Studies.

Mr. Meese spent most of his adult life working with Governor and then President Ronald Reagan. He served as the seventy-fifth Attorney General of the United States from February 1985 to August 1988. In 1985, he received the *Government Executive* magazine's annual award for excellence in management.

From 1977 to 1981, he was a Professor of Law at the University of San Diego, where he also was Director of the Center for Criminal Justice Policy and Management. Mr. Meese also served as Vice President for administration of Rohr Industries, Inc. in Chula Vista, California.

Mr. Meese graduated from Yale University in 1953 and holds a law degree from the University of California-Berkeley. He is a retired Colonel in the Army Reserve and remains active in numerous civic and educational organizations. He is the author or co-author of three books: *Leadership, Ethics and Policing; Making America Safer;* and *With Reagan: The Inside Story.* Mr. Meese and his wife, Ursula, have two grown children. They live in McLean, Virginia.

DAVID W MILLER

David W. Miller, PhD serves as the Director of the Princeton University Faith & Work Initiative (http://faithandwork.princeton.edu) and as an Associate Research Scholar and Lecturer. He is also co-founder and President of The Avodah Institute. Prior to this, he spent five years at Yale University, where he was the Executive Director of the Yale Center for Faith & Culture and taught business ethics at Yale's Divinity School and School of Management. Miller also serves as an advisor to CEOs and business leaders on issues pertaining to ethics, values, leadership, and faith at work.

Miller's first book, *God at Work: The History and Promise of the Faith at Work Movement* challenges business academics and executives, as well as theologians and clergy to think differently about the place of faith at work. Prior to academia, Miller spent sixteen years in international business and finance, the latter eight of which as a senior executive based in London, and as a partner in a small private investment banking firm. With this background, he brings a unique "bilingual" perspective to his teaching, research, and corporate advisory work.

NORM MILLER

Norm Miller, Interstate Batteries Chairman, began his career with the company shortly after graduating from North Texas State University in 1962. In the past 49 years, he has moved through the ranks of Interstate – from his father's Tennessee distributorship, to the National Field Sales team at Dallas corporate headquarters, and on to the helm of Interstate's Executive Management Team.

Miller assumed the President and Chairman roles in 1978 after working 16 years under his mentor, company-founder John Searcy. Since then, Interstate has grown to become the number one replacement battery in North America. Searcy developed the successful Interstate system of marketing, product delivery and service, and Miller expanded the team that established the current Interstate network of more than 300 distributors and 200,000 dealers across the U.S. and in Canada. Unit battery sales have steadily improved from the 1965 total of 250,000 to a world record of more than 17.0 million replacement battery sales for a twelve-month period ending this past fiscal year. In 1991, Norm relinquished the Presidency to spend more time focusing on other strategies and issues facing the company.

Additionally, Miller led the company in the founding of the Interstate Batteries Great American Race in 1983 and it has become the world's richest old car race and American's premier vintage car event. In 1989, he pioneered Interstate's entry into NASCAR racing. Teaming up with Joe Gibbs Racing in 1992, Interstate won the Daytona 500 in 1993 and the prestigious Winston Cup Championship in 2000.

1974 was a major turning point for both Miller and Interstate Batteries. It was during that year he became a Christian and changed the way he approached business and his personal life.

Through all these years and successes, Miller has maintained a commitment for spiritual development, as has the Interstate management team. As a result, Interstate encourages employees to develop fully as individuals, not just professionals. With the stress and pressures of the times, combined with those of career and family, it is crucial for people to have easy access to spiritual support. Interstate management believes the workplace is definitely included, and therefore they try to make God's love and help a priority in business.

Miller and his wife, Anne, have two children, Tracy and Scott; five grandchildren, Zach, Kyle, Braden, Grant and Matalin Anne; and one great-grandson, Jackson David.

DAVID MORKEN

David Morken is president and CEO of Bandwidth.com. In 2008, Morken was named one of the *Triangle Business Journals* 40 Under 40 top business leaders. In the same year, Bandwidth made the *Inc. Magazine* 500 list for the third consecutive year as the fourth-fastest growing privately held company and the fastest-growing telecommunications company from 2002 to 2007.

In 1994, Morken co-founded the Internet's first online tax filing service, efiling.com. He was called to active duty by the Marine Corps in 1995 and served four years as a Judge Advocate, criminal prosecutor, and headquarters company commander. Morken is a graduate of the University of Notre Dame Law School and a member of the Virginia Bar Association. He received his undergraduate degree from Oral Roberts University, where he also served as president of the student body.

Morken suffers from an addiction to endurance athletics, finishing the 2008 Wasatch 100-mile Ultra-marathon in twenty-second place with a time of less than twenty-seven hours. In 2009, *Business Leader Magazine* named Morken the Healthiest CEO in The Triangle (Raleigh-

Durham). He was the first finisher from North Carolina in the 2005 Ironman World Championships held in Kona, Hawaii, finishing in nine hours and forty-three minutes. Morken was a two-time member of the Marine Corps Triathlon team in 1997-98.

Morken resides in Chapel Hill with his wife Chrishelle and their six children.

BRIAN MOSLEY

As the President of RightNow Brian leads with a quiet and determined leadership style. He married his high school sweetheart, Julie. They have three kids, Abby, Grant and Ashley. As licensed foster parents, their home is sometimes a little fuller. They worship and serve at Allen Bible Church where Brian is also an elder. Brian graduated from Baylor University in 1999 with a film and digital media degree.

In 2000 Brian started RightNow Ministries within an existing ministry called Bluefish TV. Through some experiences in his early 20's he realized that people are longing to use their God-given passions and skills to do something significant right now. RightNow's mission is to help people trade in their pursuit of the American Dream for a world that desperately needs Christ.

RightNow has served over 110,000 churches through their video resources, leadership conferences and online training tools. The Right-Now team has worked closely with Max Lucado, Francis Chan, Erwin McManus, Matt Chandler, Doug Fields, Chip Ingram, Les and Leslie Parrott, Todd Phillips, David Nasser, Matt Carter and a host of other great teachers.

BLAKE MYCOSKIE

Blake is an entrepreneur and has created five businesses since college. His first was a successful national campus laundry service; his second start-up, Mycoskie Media, was purchased by Clear Channel Media. Between business ventures, Blake competed in the CBS' primetime series, *The Amazing Race*. With his sister, Paige, Blake traveled the world and came within minutes of winning the $1 million dollar grand prize.

After *The Amazing Race*, Blake attempted to create the first TV cable channel dedicated entirely to reality programming. His fourth start-up was an online driver's education school that featured hybrid cars and SUVs. After returning from a holiday in Argentina, Blake decided to sell this business to focus full-time on his latest idea, the creation of TOMS Shoes. TOMS Shoes focuses on the simple promise to give a pair of new shoes to children in need around the world with every pair sold.

Blake is an avid reader and traveler. He lives on a sailboat in Los Angeles.

STEVE REINEMUND

Steve Reinemund is the Dean of Business at Wake Forest University, and Professor of Leadership and Strategy. Steve retired as Chairman of the Board of PepsiCo, Inc. in May 2007 and as Chief Executive Officer in October 2006. He is a twenty-three-year PepsiCo veteran who led the corporation as Chairman and Chief Executive from 2001 to 2006. During that period, PepsiCo's revenues increased by more than $9 billion, net income increased by seventy percent, earnings per share increased by eighty percent, its annual dividend doubled, and the company's market capitalization surpassed $100 billion. In addition to the growth of the company, Steve's legacy includes a commitment to health and wellness, diversity and inclusion, and values-based leadership.

Steve is currently a member of the board of directors of American Express, Exxon, and Marriott, and serves as a trustee on the United States Naval Academy Foundation. From 2005 to 2007, Steve was chairman of the National Minority Supplier Development Council. He served on the National Advisory Board of the Salvation Army from 1990 to 1999, and he was chairman of this board from 1996 to 1999. Steve also served on the board of The National Council of La Raza from 1992 to 2001 and was chairman of its Corporate Board of Advisors from 1992 to 1996. Steve has honorary doctorates from Bryant University and Johnson and Wales University. He did his MBA at the University of Virginia and his Bachelor of Science at the United States Naval Academy.

JEFFREY A RUSSELL

Jeff is currently the CEO of Easy Office, a social venture providing affordable finance services to nonprofits in the US. He has served as the Executive Director for an international development nonprofit, The Momentum Group. He lived in Bangkok, Thailand for 3+ years as the Director of Supply Chain Planning for a $350-million supply chain services company. While there, he designed and implemented a back-office shared service center that handled over $250 million worth of transactions each year. Jeff is a Georgia Tech Industrial Engineer and holds an MBA from Yale University. He and his wife, Tara, live with their two children in Boise, Idaho.

MARK L RUSSELL

Mark L. Russell is the Founder and CEO of Russell Media. Russell is a frequent public speaker and has worked as a consultant to a wide array of organizations. He is the author of *The Missional Entrepreneur: Principles and Practices for Business as Mission* and a co-author of *Routes and Radishes: And Other Things to Talk about at the Evangelical Crossroads*. He is the editor and publisher of numerous other works and has more than one-hundred academic and popular publications.

Russell has a PhD in intercultural studies from Asbury Theological Seminary, a Master of Divinity degree from Trinity Evangelical Divinity School, and a Bachelor of Science degree in International Business from Auburn University. His PhD thesis focused on business as mission (BAM) and has been published by the Evangelical Missiological Society. Mark has lived and worked in Russia, Chile, and Germany and traveled to more than seventy countries to carry out a variety of business, educational, humanitarian, and religious projects. He has taught at numerous academic institutions in a variety of countries.

He has interviewed over 500 entrepreneurs around the world and has developed business plans in over twenty countries. Mark lives in Boise, Idaho, with his wife, Laurie and their children, Noah and Anastasia.

TYLER SELF

Tyler Self is the co-founder and Chief Investment Officer of Vision Research Capital Management, LP, a Dallas-based investment manager for accredited and institutional investors. In this role, Tyler oversees all investment activity of the firm and serves as Portfolio Manager of Vision Research Capital Fund, LP where he has built a track record of generating profitable returns that have significantly outperformed U.S. indices.

Prior to launching Vision Research Capital Fund in 2006, Tyler founded and served as CEO and Director of Research of Vision Research Organization, LLC, where he oversaw an independent consulting service targeting large institutional investors and hedge funds. Under Tyler's leadership, Vision Research was selected as the top overall Forensic Accounting, Quality of Earnings, and Short Idea research firm in the country.

Tyler graduated from Baylor University with a Bachelor of Business Administration. In the year of his graduation, Tyler was the only undergraduate student in the United States to receive direct admission to the Harvard Business School Master of Business Administration program. Tyler continues to support undergraduate education, serving on Southern Methodist University's Alternative Asset Management Center Advisory Board and frequently appearing at Baylor University as a guest lecturer.

Tyler is also active in the community, serving as a volunteer at West Dallas Community School, a director at Videre Microfinance Institution, and a teacher at his local church. Tyler and his wife Lauren have two daughters, Ava and Abigail.

JOHN TYSON

The grandson of the company's founder, Tyson Foods Chairman John Tyson has worked in the company since he was a teenager, in virtually every department, from operations to sales and marketing to governmental relations. He also served as President and CEO. Tyson was the architect of the acquisition of IBP, Incorporated in 2001, which precipitated a major change in the size and scope of the company's operations. He then structured the "new" Tyson Foods based on core values that defined goals and standards for personal and professional success.

A key part of these core values is that Tyson Foods strives to be a company of diverse people working together to produce food, which has been and continues to be a cornerstone that has supported the growth of the company throughout the years. John Tyson also created the company's first Executive Diversity Business Council to provide guidance on and support of inclusion and diversity. In recent years, Tyson has also been a leader in the concept and practice of providing company chaplains and the establishment of faith-friendly workplaces. A devoted father of two, Tyson is also engaged in supporting the well-being and education of youth. As such, he is actively involved in Tyson Foods' philanthropic efforts with a focus on education and hunger relief.

JR VASSAR

JR Vassar is the founding and lead pastor of Apostles Church in New York City, a growing and diverse Christ-centered community seeking to renew the city with the message and mercy of Christ. Apostles Church meets in two locations: Union Square and the Upper East Side of Manhattan. JR and his wife, Ginger, have three children.

FURTHER RESOURCES AVAILABLE FROM

www. RUSSELL-MEDIA.com

Do you hate budgeting? Have you found other money management systems too complex and too restrictive?

inning with Money will help you take control of your finances and start succeeding. Whether you are 18
r 58, the principles outlined inside *Winning With Money* will set you on a course of freedom, flexibility and
ictory with your money.

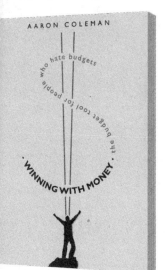

"*Winning With Money* puts the emphasis on the positive. It's not about what you can't buy; it's about having the freedom to know what you can! Coleman's approach is simple enough to stick with and flexible enough to work for any individual without making them feel like a slave to their budgeting system."

GABRIEL M. KRAJICEK
CEO, BANCVUE CORP.

"An extremely relevant book for our culture, *Winning With Money* literally changes the game for personal budgeting and finances. It puts you in control while giving you freedom to make choices and decisions that work for you. Get it today and start winning the money game."

MICHAEL GOGIS
CHIEF FINANCIAL OFFICER
WILLOW CREEK ASSOCIATION

AARON COLEMAN has worked with c-level executives throughout the United States. He specializes in helping companies operate more efficiently and profitably. He blogs regularly at winningwithmoney.com.

ARE YOU READY TO TURN YOUR ORDINARY DAY
INTO AN EXTRAORDINARY CALLING?

TRANSFORM YOUR WORK LIFE AND
TRANSFORM YOUR LIFE.

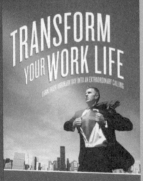

When you read the Bible, it soon becomes obvious that the focus of the ministry and outreach of Christ wa nearly exclusively in the marketplace. If you are looking for the secrets of how to succeed with your faith in your workplace, then *Transform your Work Life* is for you.

Dr. Bruce Wilkins
author of *The Prayer of Jab*

In this day and age, when anything seems to go, it is so good to know that there are still successful businessmen who operate strictly according to God's principles.

Angus Bucha
Faith like Potato

GRAHAM POWER is the founder and Board Chairman of the Power Group, one of Southern Africa's lead in the fields of civil engineering, development an deconstruction. He is also the founder of the Global Day o Prayer, a worldwide movement involving millions of people from 220 different countries.

DION FORSTER is a consultant and chaplain to the Power Group of Companies as well as the Global Day o Prayer and Unashamedly Ethical movements. Dion is an ordained minister in the Methodist Church of Sout Africa and has a doctorate of theology from the University of South Africa.

HIS BOOK TELLS THE BEST NEWS YOU WILL EVER HEAR. EVER!

The authors guarantee that your life will change for the better by the time you finish reading it. They are confident in sharing this great news, because they are not making it up. It's true.

The Best News You Will Ever Hear reports news that has changed millions and millions of people. And it reports that news in a way that you've never heard. Prepare yourself. Focus your attention and read carefully. This news should change your life for good forever!

THOMAS JAY OORD is a professor of theology, ordained minister, and author of many books. He teaches at Northwest Nazarene University in Nampa, Idaho.

ROBERT LUHN is an ordained minister and pastor of the Church of the Nazarene in Othello, Washington.

the PRESIDENTS & their FAITH

The old adage "never discuss religion and politics" is roundly rejected in this incisive exploration of Presidential history and religious faith.

The Presidents & Their Faith is a fascinating and informative look at how every U.S. president exercised their personal faith, exerted presidential power, and led a religiously diverse nation.

Has there ever been a stranger prayer than Truman's, offered upon America's successful development of the atom bomb: "We pray that He may guide us to use it in His ways and for His purposes"?

At the nation's founding, Northeast Presbyterians demanded explicit mention of Jesus in the Constitution. George Washington refuted them, saying that religious piety "was a matter best left between an individual and his God; religious instruction was the responsibility of religious societies, not the civil state." What drove Washington to make that argument, and what if he had lost?

Who wouldn't feel like the exasperated FDR when he said, "I can do almost everything in the 'Gold-fish Bowl' of the President's life, but I'll be hanged if I can say my prayers in it. It bothers me to feel like something in the zoo being looked at by all the tourists in Washington when I go to church . . . No privacy in that kind of going to church, and by the time I have gotten into that pew and settled down with everybody looking at me, I don't feel like saying my prayers at all." But even more importantly, what's real, what's a show, and why does it matter when it comes to faith and politics?

These questions and more are unpacked and examined, leading to a whole new understanding of how religion and politics interfaced through America's history, and how they will play out in our future.

In this climate of religious and political tensions, *The Presidents & Their Faith* casts a civil, yet entertaining, and insightful spotlight on the unique mix (and frequent mix-ups) of politics and religion in America.

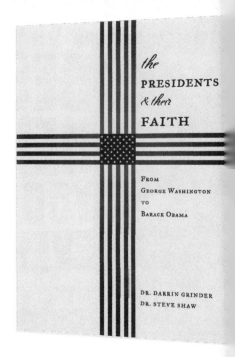

the
PRESIDENTS
& their
FAITH

From
George Washington
to
Barack Obama

Dr. Darrin Grinder
Dr. Steve Shaw

Dr. Darrin Grinder is Chair of the English Department at Northwest Nazarene University and Associate Professor of American Literature He has a Doctorate of Arts in English from Id State University. He and his wife attend Cathe of the Rockies United Methodist Church in B Idaho.

Dr. Steve Shaw is Professor of Political Scien and Director of the University Honors Program at Northwest Nazarene University. He holds th PhD degree in Political Science from the Univ sity of Oklahoma. He has taught at NNU since 1979, and he and his wife attend Holy Apostle Catholic Church in Meridian, Idaho.

FEBRUARY 2012

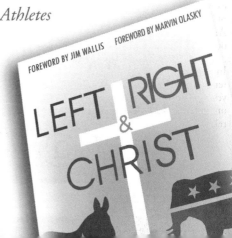

BULK ORDER DISCOUNTS FOR YOUR CHURCH OR ORGANIZATION

see

www. RUSSELL-MEDIA.com

or email

info@russell-media.com